D0560261

# UNDERSTANDING PEOPLE AT WORK

## A Manager's Guide
## to the
## Behavioral Sciences

# by Thomas L. Quick

Collages by Arnold Genkins

83-1009

*Executive Enterprises Publications Co., Inc.*
*Prentice-Hall, Inc., Englewood Cliffs, N.J. 07632*

Edited by Robert Freiberg

*Fifth Printing, 1982*

Library of Congress Cataloging in Publication Data

Quick, Thomas L.
    Understanding people at work.

    Bibliography: p.
    Includes index.
    1. Organizational behavior.    2. Industrial sociology.
3. Psychology, Industrial.    I. Title.
HD58.7.Q5 1982                158.7                81-17816
ISBN 0-917386-17-5                AACR2
ISBN 0-13-936658-X {PRENTICE-HALL}
ISBN 0-13-936641-5 {PRENTICE-HALL: PBK}

For Jan

## About the Author

At the Research Institute of America, where he is a managing editor, Thomas L. Quick is responsible for management and marketing membership publications as well as two biweeklies, *Personal Report for the Executive* and *Marketing for Sales Executives.* A graduate of Fordham University, his areas of specialization include organizational and group behavior. He lectures before business and professional groups, is a member of the American Society for Training and Development and the National Organization Development Network, and has had two previous books published: *Your Role in Task Force Management: the dynamics of corporate change* (Doubleday 1972), and *The Ambitious Woman's Guide to a Successful Career,* written with Margaret V. Higginson (AMACOM, a division of the American Management Associations).

# Contents

# Foreword

What we all once thought of as "authority" is undergoing significant changes in our society. We are moving away from authority based strictly on power and status to authority based on knowledge and ability. Today, teachers, parents, government officials, doctors, judges, and other authority figures are required to demonstrate competence in order to maintain their authority. Authority is granted by constituents to their leaders only so long as these leaders satisfy the needs and standards of the governed. This startling change applies equally to managerial authority.

Many of our concepts of managerial authority were derived from the Industrial Revolution and have been undergoing transformation ever since. Prior to that time, workers were closely associated with the product of their labors. Each person was accountable for the quantity and quality of his output. With the rise of the factory system and mass production, work became depersonalized. The management system developed in order to assure planning, execution, and control in achieving a predetermined result. The management system sharply reduced the worker's freedom and control over his work, substituting managerial judgment for that of the individual. As organizations grew, the management system expanded into a codified hierarchy whose different levels were marked by significantly different rewards and social status. Management's right to manage was based on its ownership of the means of production and on the exercise of unimpeded authority. This authority was part of the overall authority system operative in the general society.

Authority of managers was unquestioned. They could be and frequently were demanding and exploitative, and they used their authority to punish workers with impunity.

During the late 1800s, the union movement started to take hold and to challenge the free exercise of managerial authority through collective action. In many countries, socially conscious legislators began to limit managerial control over health, safety, hours, and working conditions.

With mass production and the moving assembly line, new possibilities for efficiency were discovered by conducting studies to make work more efficient. While the industrial engineers recognized that worker motivation was a key ingredient for successful productivity, workers were antagonistic to the whole efficiency movement. Workers felt they were being treated little better than machines by being manipulated and threatened with loss of their jobs by an uncaring management.

It is important to remember that developments within offices and factories are interrelated with political, economic, social, and technological changes. The waves of immigration, the emergence of socialism, expanded educational attainment, and new communications and transportation technologies have all had dramatic impact on employee attitudes, needs, and expectations.

During the late 1920s and early 1930s, pioneering work—known as "the Hawthorne studies"—was conducted by a small band of engineers and social scientists under the leadership of Elton Mayo. Previous studies of worker alienation, suicide rates among workers, and breakdowns in communications between supervisors and workers had created an awareness that the industrial system was marked by underlying resentments and tensions.

The Hawthorne studies confirmed that workers were organized on an informal basis to impede the objectives of management. An anti-authoritarian system existed as a countervailing force to managerial authority.

The insights gained during these studies have changed the focus of management action over the past forty years. It became obvious that employee cooperation was the key to productivity and achievement of corporate objectives. Cooperation cannot be mandated—it must be earned.

For managers to *earn* cooperation requires that:

- They understand the needs, attitudes, expectations, and behavior of people at work—people as both individuals and members of groups.
- They utilize this knowledge to develop specific policies, practices, and programs that will motivate employees to participate in the achievement of managerial objectives.

Significant advances have taken place since Hawthorne to help managers not only understand employee attitudes and behavior, but also elicit the cooperation and involvement required in today's world of work.

One major change has been how managers perceive and use their authority. As you read the following chapters, you will note that managerial authority today is based primarily on competence rather than edict. The old style— domineering authority figures who rule by fear—is now seen to be less effective than gaining workers' willing cooperation.

*Lewis Abrams*
Publisher

# Author's Preface

This book has been conceived and written for anyone who wants a clearer understanding of how research in the behavioral sciences is affecting and improving the quality of our working lives. Most people want to achieve objectives, their own as well as those of the organizations for which they work, in order ultimately to get more joy and satisfaction from their investment of time and energy on the job and in their relationships with others. Most of us want to know more about motivations—our own as well as other people's.

Much of the work of behavioral scientists today is devoted to studying these objectives and helping us be more effective in achieving them. Thousands and thousands of printed pages each year discuss theory and experimentation in these areas. So prodigious is the output that it is fashionable to talk about the *management-theory jungle* as if all of this effort were an impenetrable thicket in which one would easily lose all direction. But that is not accurate. There is a general direction in theory and practice. Scientists have built upon others' thinking and experiments. The results are *not* masses of contradictions and sharply differing schools of thought; there *is* a certain unity to what the research and thinking have produced.

The purpose of this book is to identify the patterns of that research and to define its direction. These pages are for the manager who wants an overview—a manager being anyone responsible for planning, organizing, controlling, or monitoring the efforts of others to achieve organizational objectives—as well as for every individual who wants a glimpse of how his or her work life is being altered by the behavioral sciences.

# Work and Morale

The Hawthorne experiments were the first major interven-
tion by behavioral scientists in industry. Management
wanted to know what factors would contribute to higher
productivity. And the Harvard University researchers
wanted to study those factors. But the scientists, under
Elton Mayo, were not prepared for what they uncovered at
the Hawthorne Works of the Western Electric Company.
(Nor did they grasp the significance of everything they did
uncover, especially the importance of social relationships
on the work scene.) In the beginning, their work was to try to
establish some relationship between conditions of work
and the incidence of fatigue and monotony among the
employees. In broad terms, the experiments consisted of
altering various factors involved in the work situation and
measuring what effects, if any, these changes had on the
workers involved.

The first experiment, which involved changing the lighting in three departments, was inconclusive. The intensity of

the lighting was varied—and production varied as well, but not always in relation to changes in the illumination.

Therefore a second experiment was set up. It involved test groups working under different illumination intensities, and a control group that had relatively constant intensity of light. Production increased in *both* test and control groups. Further research led to two conclusions: (1) The production variances were not directly related to the level of intensity of the lighting, and (2) there were apparently human factors involved that had to be studied.

The need for further study led to observations conducted over an extensive period of time. Because nothing was involved that would not be taken for granted today, the reader will be astonished to learn that these were experimental innovations at the time: Rest periods were introduced; the method of payment was changed; the workers were allowed to talk freely. In addition, rest periods and working hours were adjusted periodically. Output increased, and remained high.

The employees involved in the test were asked to give their reasons for the high production. They said that the contributing factors were the greater freedom, increased attention, decreased direct supervision, and the chance to set one's own pace. Another factor contributing to the high production rate could also have been the consequence of the employees' revised attitudes about their work: Absenteeism in the group dropped sharply.

Two other experiments were arranged to determine the role of wage incentives in increased production: These experiments took place in the second Relay Assembly Test Room and the Mica Splitting Test Room. But the relationship between more money and higher output was not easily and definitely established. Some increase in production could be assumed to follow from increased pay, but it was becoming increasingly clear to the experimenters that other factors—such as supervision—were involved. Hawthorne demonstrated that employees sometimes rated as poor supervisors whom management regarded as effective. And the employees' view of supervision was probably the more important, since they were the producers. A mass interviewing program was designed to gather from employees data that would guide supervisors in doing a better job of leadership. (Today, it is almost routine for a consultant to begin work in an organization by gathering such data and making diagnostic studies.)

Another factor that could temporarily affect production was discovered: the so-called *Hawthorne Effect.* This phenomenon has to do with the attention given a work group. During the illumination experiment, production in the control group, where lighting was kept relatively constant, went up. Similarly, during the data-gathering, many of the employees interviewed enjoyed the mere fact of the interview and benefited from it in terms of morale. Subsequent researchers and consultants have had to take this phenomenon into account in determining how much *temporary* change in morale and productivity has taken place as a result of mere attention to employees—and how much substantial, permanent modification has occurred as a result of successful efforts to change conditions and relationships. The Hawthorne Effect is an important consideration in research, since it can clutter up a project with misleading results. Response to attention may make the researcher believe that some permanent change of behavior has occurred.

## Informal Groups

Perhaps the most significant discovery of the Hawthorne team was the influence of the social or informal group upon

its members. Employees were not only economic creatures; they were social beings as well. How each felt about
work and the company—especially the group with which he
or she worked and the employee's position in the group—
had much to do with the employee's relationships with
others. The final experiment, in the Bank Wiring Observa-
tion Room, was concerned with this social or informal
group. The male employees in this room had devised
means of controlling production through ridicule, sarcasm,
and "binging"—a blow to the upper arm. If you wanted to
belong to the in group, you had to be careful not to turn out
too much or too little work; you must not harm a fellow
worker by saying anything bad about him to a supervisor.

Especially interesting is that Hawthorne management
seemed totally ignorant of the existence of such groups, a
factor that undoubtedly contributed to their maintenance
and helped to increase their power.

Because of the research done by Elton Mayo and his
team, we can assume that in every formal work group of
any size there will be at least one informal group. There are
groups formed along the lines of age, sex, experience,
seniority, and specialization. There are clusters formed by
employees who merely like to socialize with one another off
the job. Whatever the organizing principle, these informal
groups satisfy a social need in people by giving them a
sense of belonging. The formal organization, on the other
hand, is usually functional and exists—at least in
principle—for the sake of efficiency of the total operation.
Mere membership in a functional department does not automatically provide the opportunity for social satisfaction.

Writing many years after Hawthorne, Harvard's Fritz J.
Roethlisberger, an associate of Mayo, suggested that most
managements are uneasy about such groups. For one
thing, the informal groups often reflect the personal values
of the members. Consequently, management may fear a

conflict between what the organization regards as important and the priorities of employees. It isn't so much that management does not believe that employees should have personal values as it is that such values should not be expressed on the work scene—and the groups, of course, can easily be construed as a manifestation of that kind of expression.

There is no question that such groups can hold and enforce values and norms that go against those of the formal organization. The bank wiring room at the Hawthorne Works provided an example of the group setting production maximums for its members. Those who exceeded what the group felt was proper were subjected to verbal abuse and isolation. Groups can influence departmental effectiveness by making it easier or more difficult for new employees to function. If someone joins the department who is not wanted by the members of the group, they can find ways to inhibit that person's efficiency. On the other hand, what the formal organization does to help the new employee become effective can be enhanced by additional training and support given by members of the informal organization.

However, as we know since the Hawthorne experiments, an informal group may exist primarily to give members an identity, a feeling of choice and self-respect, of acceptance by others. The group may not get in the way of the workings of the formal structure. But if the members' values strongly contradict those of the organization, the group can become defensive and protective. Members can protest, or even defy, policies and norms established by the formal authority without fearing they will stand alone in doing so. It may be very difficult for a manager to discipline or discharge one or two "troublemakers" if there is reason to believe that a strong informal group exists that may provide retaliatory action in terms of a work slowdown, a rise in sick time, or even a wildcat strike.

Similarly, if management wishes to introduce a change in procedures, rules, methods, or authority, a strong informal group can find effective ways to resist the change, to slow down the adoption or transition, to make it unworkable.

The informal group poses a dilemma for the supervisor. Complete acceptance and legitimization by the supervisor may appear to be an abdication of responsibility and could mean diminution of power and authority. On the other hand, if the supervisor tries to act as if the group did not exist, he or she is risking disaffection and even retaliation.

Studies have shown that if a supervisor is to exist with a strong group, he or she should:

- Listen carefully when one member of the group is expressing a work-related opinion or giving feedback; that member could be expressing the attitudes prevalent in the group.
- Be careful when accepting newly hired people or transferring people out of the department. In the former case, it is important that the person not be totally excluded or circumvented by the group. And when people who are staunch members of the group are removed from it, they and the group may see the supervisor's action as punitive or a denial of the group's existence.
- Take special steps to obtain the group's acceptance of any important change. This usually involves preparing the group in advance, spelling out the benefits, and especially cultivating the agreement of the group leadership.

Of course, the work values of the group may well be identical with those of the formal organization, and thus there would be no need for a defensive, protective, resistant posture on the part of the group (or of management). Such a group would exist to satisfy certain *social* needs of its members, needs that are not entirely being met by participation in formal work teams.

## A Beginning

The Hawthorne Studies were terminated by the Depression, and—possibly because they were incomplete—their significance was long misunderstood by many. For one thing, it was assumed, chiefly because of the Hawthorne Effect, that there probably is a direct relationship between morale and production. This presumed relationship, not demonstrated by hard evidence, led to the belief that if management made people happy, the happiness would lead to greater output. The so-called human-relations school of management was the label given this orientation. Unfortunately, all that we definitely know about happy employees is that they are happy.

There is no question that the Hawthorne studies discovered or pointed to certain factors and relationships that have determined or heavily influenced the direction of organizational research to this day. Had they continued, they might have refined our knowledge of people's behavior in groups and of those factors that encourage greater individual productivity in teams. The studies might also have begun to deal with the existential aspects of the person— individual needs, goals, motivational factors. More than two decades were to pass before behavioral scientists could begin to impress upon us that a person's needs could be satisfied through membership in the informal *and* formal organizations. Furthermore, a worker not only is not antagonistic to the objectives of the organization but can ac-

tually pursue and gratify personal goals through attainment
of organizational objectives.

Hawthorne was a bare, almost abortive, beginning. The
next major impetus came in the 1950s, provided by the trio
of Abraham Maslow, Frederick Herzberg, and Douglas
McGregor.

# What Motivates People?

The first of the trio to publish was Abraham H. Maslow, professor of psychology at Brandeis University—and, later, president of the American Psychological Association. His book *Motivation and Personality,* published in 1954, defined a "Hierarchy of Needs." People are motivated, according to Maslow, to satisfy certain needs ranging from the very basic and bodily to the very complex and psychological. Here are the needs in ascending order of complexity:

**Physiological:** Bodily needs such as food, sex, drink, sleep;

**Safety:** The desire to be secure, to have stability, protection, freedom from fear; the need for structure and order;

**Belongingness and Love:** The wish to have friends, family, contact, intimacy;

**Esteem:** The desire to have the esteem of others as well as to feel self-esteem, to be competent and be regarded as useful, important;

**Self-Actualization:** To grow to become what one is capable of being, a process in which one's potential is realized.

Maslow says that a person feels a particular need only when the needs lower in the hierarchy are *predominantly* satisfied. Thus, a person has little drive for security or love when starving and the stomach is crying for food. The corollary is: Need that has been largely satisfied does not motivate. However, others have pointed out that a hungry artist may spend his last few dollars for tubes of paint rather than a meal. Some leaders in business, politics, etc., have been known to ignore hunger and sleep—the physiological needs—to accomplish tasks they had undertaken. Obviously, the gratification some politicians feel from shaking hands and making speeches is more powerful than what they would derive from stopping to eat or sleep. It is also possible that people can be self-actualizing while still working to satisfy lower needs.

But Maslow wasn't being rigid. He pointed out that one may make love or seek physical intimacy not only for sexual release (physiological needs) but also to achieve feelings of power over another—or even to win the esteem of others who may see the act as one of conquest. Furthermore, Maslow suggested that a need may have been satisfied for such a long time that it has become undervalued, its motivational force reduced. One may enjoy such wide esteem of others for so long that it doesn't seem important. The esteemed person may actually feel a more intense need for love of one person, which is lower in the hierarchy.

How the hierarchy works specifically—*if* it does (and numerous experiments to demonstrate its validity had inconsistent results)—is probably not a terribly important consideration. Maslow did not intend the scheme to be rigid and comprehensive. He was hardly saying, "This is the way behavior is; there is no other explanation." Furthermore, it is sometimes very difficult to translate general needs into specific objectives. If we are to understand what motivates people, then we must know what objectives they are working to attain at a given time. For example, it is not enough to say that Mary Phillips works hard as a secretary because she seeks esteem. The significant question is, *whose* esteem? That of her boss? That of other secretaries with whom she feels competitive? The answer might be both, depending on the task she is engaged in.

What undoubtedly was most important in 1954 was the recognition that people—individual human beings—have needs they strive to fill, that those needs are complex, and that the needs a person is trying to satisfy today may be quite different from those motivating him tomorrow or her next week. Needs in people vary from day to day, task to task, situation to situation. The implications for anyone who supervised the work of others were enormous, obviously. The hierarchy threatened much of the foundation of traditional management practice.

Interestingly, Maslow's approach—in the era of the so-called Organization Man—became rather popular. His humanism and his ability to relate to people undoubtedly have much to do with that popularity. But what is probably the most attractive aspect of the hierarchy is a need different from the other needs in the hierarchy: self-actualization. Self-actualization is the process of achieving one's potential, of becoming what one is capable of being. People respond to deficits where the other needs are concerned. They don't have enough food, or esteem, or love. So they work to acquire them. They don't have a choice. But Maslow sees people seeking to actualize themselves not out of a deficiency but to complete a stage in their growth. Some people never really reach this stage; hence, they are never impelled to begin the process of self-actualization.

Self-actualizing people accept themselves. They don't become defensive about their shortcomings, and they don't allow themselves to be self-satisfied about their virtues. The self-actualizers are spontaneous (not studied), natural, concerned with basic issues rather than with trivia or the arcane. Undoubtedly their naturalness and high self-acceptance help them to interrelate well with others; they tend to form deep relationships with a few people, not many.

People at the self-actualizing level of development enjoy solitude and privacy. They are independent and able to govern themselves. They work for material rewards, but many other kinds as well—satisfaction in doing a good job, a sense of accomplishment, pride, a desire to grow, development of skills and talents. They are alert to what is going on around them. They frequently see new things—or old things in a fresh way. They are creative and problem-centered rather than self-centered.

Self-actualizing individuals are very attractive, and very pleasant to be around. Who wouldn't want to *be* one? However, the need to self-actualize is bound to cause problems for most people in most organizations, where the autonomy of the self-actualizer is difficult to achieve and where the opportunities to develop—to actualize—so many talents are severely limited. Perhaps it is realistic to say that a person in organizational life is more often "actualized" according to the needs of the organization than to his or her own.

The humanism of Abraham Maslow began to break barriers and molds. In the better-educated, newly affluent working population of the 1950s and early 1960s there was a growing need to shed the perception of people as economic animals, working only for subsistence and material gain. The notion that people had other kinds of needs they worked to satisfy, needs that were within them and could be satisfied by rewards that were inherent in the work they performed, appealed to many.

## Theory X-Theory Y

People perceive themselves as complex beings, responding to various—and ever more exalted—needs. This perhaps explains the almost instant acceptance of the thinking of a man who was himself heavily influenced by Abraham Maslow. Douglas McGregor's book *The Human Side of Enterprise* made its appearance in 1960 and achieved a tremendous impact. McGregor, a professor at Massachusetts Institute of Technology and a former president of Antioch College, became famous for his Theory X and Theory Y.

Each theory, as McGregor defined it, is a set of assumptions that are made about people in general. Each is the way some of us look at humanity. Theory X is traditional and quite familiar:

1. The average human being has an inherent dislike of work and will avoid it if he can.
2. Because of this human characteristic of dislike of work, most people must be coerced, controlled, directed, threatened with punishment to get them to put forth adequate effort toward the achievement of organizational objectives.
3. The average human being prefers to be directed, wishes to avoid responsibility, has relatively little ambition, wants security above all.

McGregor did not mean Theory X to reflect how people actually are. Rather, it has to do with how people are viewed by others. Those managers who see people through a

Theory X lens probably suspect that humans view Eden as the ideal state: Adam and Eve did not have to work. Work is a punishment for Adam's sin. Thus it takes even greater punishment, or the threat of it, to make people perform on the job. Rather than work, people would prefer to loaf and do nothing. The effective organization, the one that achieves worker productivity adequate to meet its objectives, can do so only with elaborate controls that let people know they can't get away with not working. Probably the best way to treat employees is as children: They need a responsible parent upon whom they can be dependent and who will make sure they do what they should do.

Theory Y is another way of looking at people. It is not the other end of the spectrum. Theory X and Theory Y do not make up the total perspectives of people; they reflect two different sets of values. The following is Douglas McGregor's description of Theory Y:

1. The expenditure of physical and mental effort in work is as natural as in play or rest.
2. External control and the threat of punishment are not the only means for bringing about effort toward organizational objectives. Man will exercise self-direction and self-control in the service of objectives to which he is committed.
3. Commitment to objectives is a function of the rewards associated with achievement of those objectives.
4. The average human being learns, under proper conditions, not merely to accept but to seek responsibility.
5. The capacity to exercise a relatively high degree of imagination, ingenuity, and creativity in the solution of organizational problems is widely, not narrowly, distributed in the population.

6. Under the conditions of modern industrial life, the intellectual potentialities of the average human being are only partially utilized.

Theory Y sees people having to work not because someone is making them, but because it is built into them as human beings. It is natural. People work not to avoid something—punishment, for example—but to achieve something that is valuable to them. As Theory Y views people, they don't seek to be dependent upon and controlled by others in all that they do; they actually seek responsibility so as to have some control over their own efforts (a theme that is to become increasingly important in the behavioral sciences and work). The effective organization is not so much one that creates controls and penalties as it is one that tries to remove the obstacles to better performance by the people who are part of the organization.

Maslow had suggested that people have needs, and that they work to satisfy those personal needs. McGregor took the motivation theory further and said that people will work *in a job* to achieve objectives to which they are committed. It takes only a short jump to assume that people can identify with the goals of the organization. People can achieve personal rewards through fulfillment of organizational objectives.

McGregor's Theory Y had appeal: The needs Maslow saw in people were relevant on the job because those needs could be satisfied—at least in part—by working in an organization. Now managers were beginning to think they had a new handle on "motivating" subordinates.

Thus, during the 1960s it became commonplace—though erroneous—to speak of Theory X or Theory Y management. If managers tended to be autocratic, tough, task-oriented; if they declined to trust employees to work on their own without constant, skeptical supervision; if they took it for granted people would cheat, lie, take shortcuts rather than put out a fair day's work, then they were labeled Theory X managers, or the leadership style reflecting any of the above was termed Theory X management.

Theory Y management in contrast was open and trusting, democratic as opposed to autocratic, concerned with people, extending authority and responsibility further down in the organization, involving employees in decisions that affect them and their work. Human relations became a familiar, honored term.

Some of these interpretations given to Theory X-Theory Y distressed McGregor. He had attempted to formulate two particular views of people, views that reflected assumptions that were held about human beings. X and Y were points on a continuum extending through all views of humankind. McGregor was not attempting to give a definitive description of people, their motivations, their attitudes toward work. Nor was he under any illusion that he was producing the ultimate management manual (which many assumed would be based on Theory Y).

The mistake that produced this illusion of a management style has always been with us in industrial society: People are seen as members of groups, in general. Labels tend to be applied indiscriminately. Exchanging one set of assumptions about humanity for another doesn't necessarily result in going from an ineffective management style to an effective one. Such a move perpetuates a hit-or-miss tradition of managing people. There are, in any organization, some people who want more direction and some who want less. There are employees who take pleasure in being creative and innovative; there are those who feel no need or inclination to be so. Some people derive their greatest satisfactions from activities off the job; they regard work as the way of subsidizing those outside interests. Many jobs are boring. They have to be tolerated—but not enjoyed. Some human beings are psychologically dependent upon others; others are autonomous and prefer to direct themselves.

The importance of Theory X and Theory Y is two-fold. In the first place, stating the theory gave form to certain perspectives that had been in existence but had never before been articulated in a scientific manner; second, McGregor made it "respectable" to think in terms of people achieving personal objectives through their efforts to help organizations achieve theirs. The work itself could, therefore, be a powerful motivator.

## The Two-Factor Theory

No one has done more to emphasize work itself as a potential motivator than Frederick Herzberg. Maslow defined those common needs in us that we strive to satisfy. McGregor suggested that at least some of those needs could be satisfied on the job and through attainment of organizational objectives. Herzberg believed that people can be motivated by the work itself, that accomplishing organizational tasks and objectives fulfills a human need, and that job content can be varied to provide a greater or a lesser motivating force, depending partly on its degree of challenge.

Professor Herzberg, formerly at Carnegie Institute of Technology, then at Case-Western Reserve, and more recently at the University of Utah, based his concept of "job enrichment"—a major contribution—on what is called the two-factor theory, the components of which are job satisfiers and dissatisfiers. First advanced in the 1959 book *The Motivation to Work,* and fleshed out in *Work and the Nature of Man,* published in 1966, the theory describes job satisfiers, or motivators. The following are considered by Herzberg to be motivators:

**Achievement:** The successful completion of a job or task; a solution; the results of one's work;

**Recognition of achievement:** An act of praise or some other notice of the achievement;

**Work itself:** Tasks as sources of good feelings about it; extent of duties;

**Responsibility:** For one's own work or that of others; new tasks and assignments;

**Advancement:** An actual improvement in status or position;

**Possibility for growth:** Potential to rise in the organization.

These are the factors that motivate and satisfy people, that encourage them to want to work—and to work well. The presence of any of these factors will satisfy or motivate; however, their absence will not necessarily demotivate or cause dissatisfaction.

According to Herzberg, there is another set of influences on how an employee views the job: dissatisfiers (also called hygiene or maintenance factors). They don't motivate. Their presence won't provide job satisfaction. Their absence, however, will create dissatisfaction:

• *Supervision:* Its quality is determined by willingness or unwillingness to teach or to delegate responsibility; differences in leadership can result in things running smoothly or being irritating;

• *Company policy and administration:* Structure, good or bad communications, adequate or inadequate authority, harmful or beneficial effects of company and personnel policies;

• *Positive working conditions:* environmental and physical conditions;

• *Interpersonal relations with peers, subordinates, and superiors:* The social and working transactions with others on the job;

• *Status:* How one's position or standing is perceived by others; perquisites of rank;
  • *Job security:* Stability, tenure;
  • *Salary:* Compensation;
  • *Personal life:* How aspects of the work—such as long hours, or required transfer and relocation—affect the employee's personal life.


Herzberg's research threatened to poke holes in many popular beliefs. For these maintenance factors are not impellers. People are not motivated by bright, cheery, well-lighted work places. A pleasant supervisor does not automatically provide motivation. Despite a long-prevailing view, it seems that people are not driven to attain job security.

Herzberg's ideas found early acceptance. Some cynics have claimed that downgrading of the importance of salary from its traditional role of "nearly sole motivator" to "hygiene factor with no motivating power" was very attractive to managements not willing to pay any more than they were forced to  However, what employees were expressing to Herzberg and his associates was that they don't work for the dollars as such. Presumably everyone likes money, and if there isn't enough of it, people become unhappy. But an employee isn't motivated to achieve greater work output by being given a raise in dollars earned.

Salary, however, can play an important role as a symbol of recognition of achievement, for, in Herzberg's terms, such recognition *is* a motivator. Also, salary can be linked so closely with growth and advancement that it may be difficult to distinguish between it as a satisfier or a dissatisfier. The varied roles of money in motivation have not been thoroughly studied. It may be that dollars have a direct short-term rather than long-term influence. For example, the person who is led to believe in October that special effort will result in a large raise could conceivably be motivated to work hard to get the extra money. However, once the raise has been granted, the money is no longer a motivator. Herzberg would say the hygiene value has dropped to zero. No motivators, no dissatisfaction.

Money is not the only ambiguous dissatisfier. Surroundings may not motivate, but a large, cheery, corner office may—as recognition of achievement. Supervision does not act as a motivator, but a supervisor can provide motivating factors: growth opportunities and increased responsibilities.

A serious question raised by Herzberg's research is the relationship between job satisfaction and motivation. Unquestionably there is a connection. But what is lacking is solid evidence showing that, when people are the beneficiaries of those conditions that they say satisfy them—when those expressed motivating factors are present in the work and the environment—increased productivity is the result. No such data were in the original research, which has been criticized for having had too narrow a base. Many researchers feel the work done by Herzberg and his colleagues reflects too little time and too few people, considering the enormous importance of the hypotheses. Just as in the case of Maslow's theory, subsequent attempts by others to confirm the results of Herzberg's project have not always been satisfactory.

Nevertheless, the two-factor theory confirmed the trend in motivation thinking: people *can* satisfy needs through work and through helping organizations achieve their goals. Out of this has come an effort to make work more satisfying, more rewarding for employees—for example, through *job enrichment*—i.e., through changing the nature and responsibilities of a job to provide greater growth and challenge. The concept and practice of job enrichment is discussed elsewhere in this book.

Few managers had problems accepting Herzberg's premise that most of their rewards came from doing their work well and getting ahead with their careers. The time had come for this type of thinking. In an affluent society such as we had in the 1960s, with a work force composed of people who knew there were job and career options and who enjoyed mobility and security because of a nearly full employment situation, people did not have to settle for "a job"—instead, they sought pleasing, satisfying work. Maslow, McGregor, and Herzberg became a widely quoted trio.

Their contributions were innovative and seminal. And they were timely: There was need for a new way of looking at people. Many found the theories personally useful (perhaps true of most of those who became supporters). They could identify certain motivating factors in themselves. It was not hard to see that large numbers of managers were quite willing to believe they, and perhaps some of their bosses and peers, fit Theory Y assumptions. They saw themselves as really more concerned with the work itself—as self-actualizers, in Maslow's terms. However, these same managers were not always ready to believe that their subordinates were similarly motivated. In fact, many who saw themselves in Theory Y terms still viewed subordinates as justifying Theory X assumptions.

But in truth—and in all fairness—it was very difficult as a manager to apply the theories. How does a manager know with any assurance what need in the hierarchy of needs an employee is working on at a given time? Maslow said that when one need was predominantly taken care of we move on to the next higher one. But it's probably true that most of us are working on more than one need at any time.

Furthermore, however much one may believe that people prefer working to doing nothing, that they quite naturally display creativity on the work scene, it is a bit risky to base one's management style strictly on Theory Y assumptions.

There are employees who show much more innovativeness in off-the-job activities than on. There are people who would rather fish and hunt than work on an assembly line—or anywhere else, for that matter. Some people don't strive to shape their jobs to their own specifications, don't demand more responsibility, actually like to have their activities monitored. There are employees who cannot be trusted to make responsible, honest use of an employer's time or property.

It is probably true that everyone responds to broad, vaguely defined needs. But those needs may be hard to recognize. Much of the early motivational thinking tried to categorize these needs. But the plain fact is that managers didn't know what to do with this kind of thinking. It sounded good and it read well. But much more help was needed—specific, pragmatic help. Managers needed guidelines, and some were provided in the work of two other psychologists in the 1960s and 1970s.

## Value and Expectancy—Vroom and Rotter

It may not be possible for today's managers to have all of the answers to what motivates the people who report to them. But managers should at least know the right *questions.* And some very helpful ones have been developed in the research of two Connecticut psychologists, working independently: Victor Vroom of Yale University and Julian Rotter of the University of Connecticut. Both have relied on experimental methods to develop their models of behavior. Both have published their theories and the results of their empirical research.

The work of Vroom and Rotter can be briefly described in these terms: People will usually consider two questions in choosing a course of action. The first has to do with value of the action: How important is *this* goal to me as opposed to *that* one? The young college graduate ponders whether to get a graduate degree in business administration or to start a career immediately. The manager looks at the in-box and wonders whether he will go through its contents or whether he will work on the plan for departmental reorganization first. Which course of action looks more rewarding at this time? Which course holds the greater reward or gratification at this moment? In each case, say Rotter and Vroom, the value of the reward to the individual for doing a thing will play a large part in whether one prefers outcome *A* to outcome *B*.

Vroom defines this preference for an outcome as *valence.* He makes the point that the individual's preference for a particular outcome may extend beyond the immediate consequence of an action to that which happens later. For example, a person may accept a dinner invitation with the boss in lieu of playing tennis with a friend. The dinner invitation is not really preferable, nor is the conversation with the boss. But possible advancement may eventually result from the dinner as a consequence of the impression that the employee makes. This is the ulterior outcome that *is* preferred.

But the value of the reward is only part of the decision-making process. The other critical question concerns the person's expectation of actually achieving the outcome: Will I be able to have the reward I prefer? Sheila may not take the attractive offer from the other firm because she feels she has certain inadequacies in technical knowledge they will expect her to have. The pay may be much better than she has at present, the promotion opportunities greater, the position more prestigious than the one she occupies now. But the risk of failure is higher than if she stays where she is.

A manager may try to enhance the value of an assignment for an employee by saying, "If you do this successfully, I shall promote you to supervisor." The superior may have made the work more valuable, true. But the employee may not believe the manager has the authority to promote—or may not trust the manager to keep his or her word. Therefore, in the subordinate's eyes, the probability of being successful in reaching the goal is vastly reduced.

There are many factors that influence a person's expectancy of a successful outcome. Obviously, there must be a cause-and-effect relationship in the person's mind. The perceived ability of the person to influence the outcome is paramount: If I do this, that will occur. People often feel that their ability to affect conditions is impaired because of inadequate training or education: I want to do this, but I'm not sure I know how. Or they may feel a lack of control because of external factors—weather, interference by others, the economy, unpredictable equipment, etc.

In addition, says Rotter, the *situation* can affect how an employee may view the value of the choice and its outcome. A young, ambitious salesperson may be lusting for a branch managership. But when the vacancy turns out to be in a small rural community three hundred miles from anywhere, he may lose interest. The value has just been reduced. The young systems analyst is thrilled with the invitation to join the task force that will determine division reorganization, until she discovers that the task force leader is a person who, she feels, will not permit her to work effectively and with whom she will have much conflict. Both the value of the assignment and her expectancy of success in it have been reduced.

Vroom believes that the action taken by a person will correspond to the strongest force, a force that is the product of the outcome's valence times the strength of the expectancy that the outcome will occur. Other researchers report that they have had trouble confirming this equation. It would be difficult for someone who is trying to influence another's choice of action or behavior—a manager, say—to determine the strength of the force in the other person's mind. One complication that comes to mind is the so-called *gambler's fallacy*: the expectancy may not be strong but the payoff is so great that the risk is taken, even though the odds against may be one thousand to one. Or a person may have such an emotional investment in the outcome of an action that nothing can dissuade him from attempting it despite only slight chances of success.

Nevertheless, Vroom's expectancy theory and Rotter's social learning theory offer the manager some substantial guidelines. These continue in the tradition that behavior is goal-oriented: People do things to achieve something. Those who supervise the work of others and are concerned about motivating them can take steps to enhance the value of a task, function, or assignment. They can also expedite the success of other people's efforts.

The manager needs to ask questions, or to observe behavior in the context of those questions. For example: Is this the kind of work the employee likes, feels gratified in doing, rewarded in achieving? Is there another kind of work the employee finds more rewarding? Are there obstacles in the way of that achievement? Does the employee anticipate problems that are roadblocks to successful performance, or to success in more generalized terms? Are there factors in the environment, people, location, or physical features of the work that make it less valuable or that increase the risk of failure?

Knowing the right questions to consider—and to ask— can point the manager in the right, effective direction. There are a number of ways the value of a job can be enhanced with money, prestige, advancement, etc. Many resources are available—training, equipment, professional expertise—and the availability of a manager—to increase the employee's feeling that he can do the work handily.

Of course, approaching the matter of motivation this way means a great amount of work. Each employee, after all, has his or her own values. Each has differing abilities. The manager has to get involved on a personal, individual level, increasing the complexity of his job. And it requires continuing attention, because people, work, values, and conditions change.

The chief point—and an encouraging one—for managers is that the expectancy model and the social learning theory offer more than just explanations. They also offer ways managers can affect those around them for the better. We are not restricted to passively understanding what goes into motivation—now we can actively influence the motivating forces in people. By increasing the value of the rewards, or by furnishing greater resources, or by making the situation more congenial, managers can improve the chances that a motivated and committed employee will show better results in working toward organizational goals. Some techniques for accomplishing these steps will be discussed in the following pages.

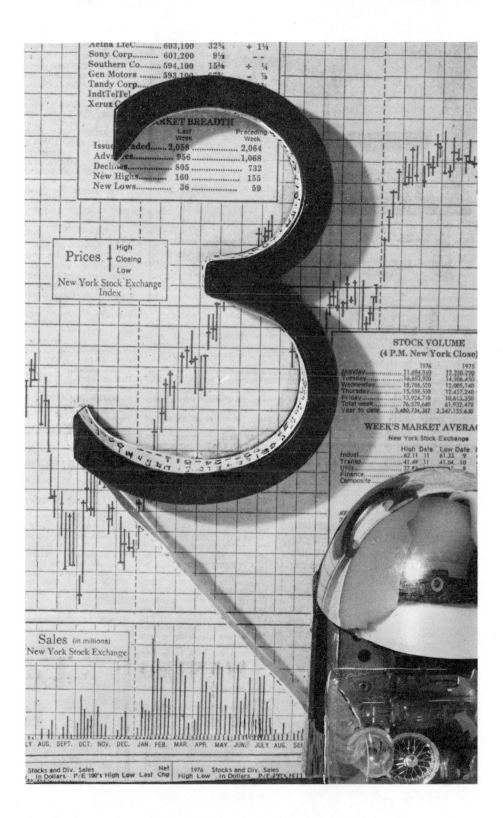

# Helping People Increase Their Motivation

Many of the theories discussed in the preceding pages have, at least in part, in one form or another, been put to the test in organizations. As previously mentioned, underlying most of the practical applications of motivation theory is acceptance of the belief that behavior is goal-oriented. In exercising a choice of what course to follow, in performing functions consciously, people are working to achieve a goal, something that is meaningful to them. For most people, work has a purpose, and in recent years, enlightened management has searched for ways to help employees reach their objectives through the attainment of *organizational* goals. It is a complex task. No two people have exactly the same objectives, no two will always respond in exactly the same way to any particular reward for doing good work.

## Reward system

We should identify and distinguish between two basic kinds of rewards. *Intrinsic* rewards flow from the actual performance of a task. There is a sense of fulfillment, an increase of self-esteem from the accomplishment itself, from the demonstration of professional and technical skill that the work involved, or from aesthetic satisfaction. *Extrinsic* rewards, on the other hand, are conferred by others. These rewards may include money, recognition, praise, and promotion.

Both kinds are important. Achievement as well as recognition of achievement are among Herzberg's motivators. Maslow describes both extrinsic and intrinsic rewards in his hierarchy, although the highest need, self-actualization, presumably is intrinsic. Most social scientists would undoubtedly recommend that if an organizational reward system is to encourage repeated good performance by employees, it should be a combination of intrinsic and extrinsic rewards.

Actually, most organizations probably do an inadequate job with either type. Most people find themselves doing the same kind of tasks over and over, and thus they are unlikely to feel a substantial sense of accomplishment. The work done by most employees is assigned by the organization without any regard for the employees' sense of self-fulfillment from doing the task. Thus, for many people, job content may provide little opportunity for intrinsic rewards. To remedy this deficiency, the work should at least:

- Be challenging enough so that the worker feels some sense of accomplishment from having completed the assignment;
- Offer results that satisfy an employee's personal objectives—for example, a sense of growth and progress, an expansion of skills and knowledge, etc.

- Be divisible so that a worker is truly identifiable with the finished product or task.

The presence of those three conditions is difficult to ensure in many organizations, given their bureaucratic structures and the narrowly defined functions and carefully rationed power of the hierarchical, pyramidal form.

Of course, the administration of extrinsic rewards is complicated. Take money as an example. For maximum effectiveness, a reward should follow as closely as possible in time the achievement that it recognizes. And yet, merit increases are awarded at intervals that suit the convenience of the organization rather than the occurrence of employees' achievements. Thus, because of a time lag, merit increases may not achieve their fullest effect.

Money in Herzberg's theory is not by itself a motivator. But even if that supposition is correct, it is obvious that money means different things to different people. Money can offer status and prestige, opportunity for luxuries and off-the-job interests, proof of success, freedom, and power, to cite but a few meanings. This same variation in individual perception is also characteristic of other extrinsic rewards: fringe benefits such as insurance, pensions, vacations, sick time; education and training; relocation to a desirable place to live; promotion, responsibility, power, and influence; publicity; more interesting assignments.

A reward system therefore includes far more than money. It should provide the kinds of work that are meaningful and important to employees—and then reward them significantly for significant achievement. For example, let us suppose that merit increases in pay may not exceed 8%. However, each department head might have a special budget allowance that provides for a bonus for exceptional performance.

The other cutting edge of the blade is this: An informal

reward can contradict a formally articulated policy. For example, there could be an organization that has an affirmative-action program to promote women and minorities but that, in reality, quietly rewards supervisors who are "clever" enough to circumvent the program without exposing the organization to legal action.

A reward system can be undermined by a great disparity between the formal and informal. If people are to work hard to seek rewards important to them, they need to know what those rewards are, and they must have a reasonable assurance of winning the rewards if they satisfy the conditions for doing so.

## The Scanlon Plan

One interesting—and successful—effort to tie extrinsic rewards to high performance by employees is the Scanlon Plan. This is a specific and systematic plan to provide extrinsic rewards for employees' efforts to increase productivity and profits. It is the brainchild of the late Joseph N. Scanlon, a union official who became an instructor at the Massachusetts Institute of Technology. Scanlon envisioned a system in which the people who actually do the work and know it best can have the opportunity to find ways to do it more efficiently, to present those improvements for consideration, and to be rewarded if more efficiency results from the implementation. The Scanlon Plan differs from a suggestion system in that Scanlon rewards are distributed to the entire group involved in the work rather than to an individual who originates the idea.

In profit sharing, by contrast, workers may receive a bonus without knowing why they are getting it or without having participated in the decisions or plans that led to the increased profit. For example, irrespective of productivity, the sale of a division may produce a large profit that is reflected in the year-end bonus. Very often, too, there is such a time lag between contribution to profits and bonus as a reward for that contribution that workers do not see the connection.

Scanlon-Plan rewards are usually distributed monthly or quarterly. At the very heart of the plan is the *production committee,* meeting at least once a month (more often, if necessary). Made up of representatives of labor and management, the committee discusses ways of cutting down or eliminating waste, more efficient methods of getting the work out, scheduling, and any other factors that might lead to improvements and lower costs. It is to the production committee that suggestions to be considered come from employees or groups of employees. (Ideally, managers and supervisors on the lower levels should be evaluated on the basis of the quantity and quality of suggestions submitted by the employees who report to them.)

The foundation of a Scanlon Plan is the "normative" labor cost, a standard by which improvements can be measured. For example, suppose the normal payroll equals 38% of production costs; if the payroll were reduced in a month, the amount saved would be the bonus. To illustrate:

| Production costs | $100,000 |
|---|---|
| Normal payroll (38%) | 38,000 |
| Actual payroll | 35,000 |
| | $ 3,000 bonus |

(Holiday and vacation payments are not included in payroll figures.)

Each month or quarter, depending upon the established frequency of bonus payments, the screening committee (also made up of labor and management)—to which the minutes of each production committee are sent—determines from actual figures for the preceding period what the bonus—or deficit—is. All suggestions accepted by production committees are recorded, all those rejected

are reviewed. In addition, the screening committee discusses anything that might affect the plan, such as problems in the sales force or strikes that may slow or hamper
distribution. Management may reserve the right to accept
or reject any suggestion adopted by a production committee.

In some plans, the entire bonus may go to the production
force. In others, 75 percent goes to workers, 25 percent to
the company. Usually a reserve is set up whereby a portion
of the bonus is put aside to cover periods in which there
might be an increase in payroll costs, hence a deficit. However, some companies make it a policy to absorb deficits. If
the plan administers a reserve, this may also be distributed
periodically—say, at the end of twelve months—as an additional bonus after the deficits are taken care of.

Proponents of the Scanlon Plan make the following
arguments in favor of this kind of bonus-sharing: the
emphasis is on efforts by the group, where, they say, goal-
setting is most meaningful. It encourages initiative and collaboration among employees. The plan reduces resistance
to change, since that change is advocated bilaterally by
labor and management instead of being dictated from on
high. Most important, perhaps, is that people who make a
special effort see a reward for that effort, a reward which is
clearly connected to improved efficiency.

Scanlon plans have been in effect for a number of years,
and executives of most companies using them feel they
have developed significant performance figures to show
that installation of the plan pays off. Still, the Scanlon Plan
has never become widely accepted in American industry.

## Job Enrichment

If the Scanlon Plan is designed to increase the effectiveness of *extrinsic* rewards, job enrichment is an approach to

enhance *intrinsic* ones. The practice of job enrichment is the child of Herzberg's two-factor theory of job satisfaction translated into reality in such pioneering efforts as those of Robert Ford at AT&T and of M. Scott Myers at Texas Instruments. Recall that people are motivated by the work itself, by advancement and growth. But the work cannot provide a sense of progress if it does not at least match the ability of employees to do it. Boring, monotonous, easy work can be demeaning.

The purpose and rationale of job enrichment is to put challenge into a job, to provide growth and advancement for the employee who wants it and can handle it. Thus we see a trend away from the functionalism and work simplification in which the job is broken down into the simplest, most mechanical units that nearly anyone can perform adequately (sometimes without having to think about it). In job enrichment, employees may, as an example, actually undertake to assemble a complete unit of something rather than, as before, operate as an assembly line with each person having a small responsibility in the sequence.

A number of terms are often mistakenly used synonymously in connection with changing tasks to relieve monotony or to provide broader duties (which generally became known as job redesign). These terms are rotation, enlargement, and enrichment. Job rotation provides an employee with experience in a number of functions; he spends a certain time in this one, and then time in that one, and so on. The term is relevant in this discussion although, strictly speaking, it is not job enrichment. The person in a job-rotation program may not always be acquiring skill in new functions; the purpose may simply be to gain exposure to the other jobs.

In the case of *job enlargement,* however, employees are exposed to other responsibilities and functions in order to become capable of doing them. Thus, a file clerk might take on stenographic duties. The extra work assigned is usually *on the same level* of responsibility as the primary or original duties of the jobholder. Job enlargement, for that reason, is often called *horizontal loading*—although the work is new to the employee, it comes from the same level he or she is accustomed to.

Job enrichment, however, is referred to as *vertical loading,* for what is added comes from a higher level of responsibility. An employee would not only do the job assigned to his or her usual level, but he or she might take over the planning, scheduling, or control functions of the job as well.

Prior to enrichment, these traditionally have been the province of the supervisor. A typist might assume the responsibility of checking for typing errors, a function formerly performed by her supervisor. People on an assembly line might take over quality inspection of their own work. Cleaning crews might form teams and allocate tasks among the members.

The installation of a job-enrichment program often starts with an orientation program (including reassurance) for supervisors whose employees are to have their jobs enriched. Much of the loading for the employees' new responsibilities will come from the supervisory level, so it is necessary to avoid threatening the supervisors' sense of security. (Supervisors might otherwise see the job-enrichment program as the first step in eventually doing away with their level of management.) The supervisors may be able to suggest how some of their planning and control functions can be transferred to lower levels. (The chances are that the supervisors, when promoted, brought with them certain functions and duties from the lower levels at the time of promotion, favored duties that they were reluctant to give up and leave behind.)

The next step is to consult the people whose jobs will be most affected by the change. How do they believe their jobs can be improved and enriched?

In many organizations the enrichment effort has largely

been confined to the lower levels. But really effective enrichment should take place on each level of the hierarchy right up to the top, if only because employees and managers at every level are undoubtedly spending valuable time and effort performing tasks and functions that could as easily, and more properly, be accomplished at lower levels. Few people at any rank in the average organization are in danger of being used at or near capacity. Most are underutilized, and a job-enrichment effort is one approach to correcting this waste of human ability.

Giving people more say about what they do and how they do it, providing them with more control over their work, putting more responsibility and learning opportunities in the lower levels: All these steps should increase the effectiveness and the motivational forces in employees affected. But it doesn't always happen that way. Here are some pitfalls:

- Some people don't *want* their job enriched. The problem begins when someone in the organization—or outside, as in the case of a consultant—decides that a given job is boring and monotonous. But that is a subjective judgment. The person holding the job may be quite happy with the way things are. The assumption that everyone needs to be enriched is sometimes counterproductive.

- Employees at lower levels are often told how their jobs are to be altered without their being consulted. The enrichment thereby begins to resemble any other kind of change in which employees worry about what is being done to them or how they are being manipulated.

- The enrichment program is sometimes instituted without a change in the reward system. Merely being told "You will benefit from the changes," people cannot be blamed for feeling that management has devised a scheme to get more out of them for less pay.

Once again, as with any major new program, there must be a continuing commitment—from the top down—to the changes being made. Every person affected by the program should be comprehensively informed as to what is taking place, and why—preferably with a spelling out of benefits to the individual. People should have their jobs enriched at a pace that suits them and their capabilities. There must be ample opportunity for feedback to higher management as the program matures. Finally, if management enriches jobs and expects employees to do more work and assume greater responsibility, there should be provision for higher rewards to reflect these changes.

## Managing by Objectives

Management by objectives (or results), generally known as MBO, is an attempt to formulate on a systematic, system-wide basis the goals and objectives that can play such important roles in motivating people to more effective performance. The concept is credited to Peter Drucker, management consultant, author, and professor. As an approach to better management, the impetus for MBO has, to a great extent, been provided by George Odiorne in the U.S. and John Humble in the United Kingdom. Its inclusion here is easily understood: MBO recognizes and utilizes some of the most potent concepts and research findings of the social scientist of the past three decades.

MBO has become immensely popular in the United States for a number of reasons. First of all, it seems born of common sense: Plan what you propose to do within a time period and then monitor your progress. It is simple—deceptively so. Many people have been doing something like it for many years (it is not uncommon to hear an experienced supervisor protest that MBO presents nothing new). So there is a familiarity. MBO seems to fill the interstices uncovered by the psychological research of recent years. People *can* be motivated to achieve. Herzberg's two-factor theory maintains that people are motivated by the work itself, by achievement, and by recognition of achievement. The learning theorists tell us that people need feedback in order to be motivated to learn and acquire skills. All of these are supplied by MBO. Here you are now; here's where you want to be one year hence; here's how you will know you are there; etc.

Of course, MBO is ideal for organizations. It helps management to plan, to set goals for the organization, to formulate strategy. Here is the overall goal; here is the goal broken down for each unit of operation. Management not only can see who is going to contribute what, but also can satisfy itself that all units in the organization are brought into the planning and understand the total objectives. Furthermore, people are more likely to commit themselves to objectives they themselves have helped to formulate.

The basic premises and procedures of management by objectives are, as has been said, deceptively simple. The popular view of MBO resembles this: Top management defines the overall goals for the coming year. These goals are communicated down the line to managers, and the question is asked: "What can you and your department do to help us achieve these goals?" The managers then set *their* objectives to implement contributing to the organizational goals. The people at the top look at the aggregate of all of this goal-setting, make sure it all adds up to the large organizational goals, and then ask managers and employees at all levels to commit themselves to the objectives already spelled out. At the end of the year, assuming no unexpected setback or crisis has occurred, the organizational goals should have been achieved.

Disappointingly often, this is not the case. To understand why so many MBO systems fail, we should first look at the components that are recommended for inclusion in an MBO program:

1. Position analysis or description, which outlines the areas of responsibility and accountability;
2. The objectives for the position—what is to be achieved by one performing the functions outlined in the position analysis;
3. Setting objectives jointly with a superior so that they are agreed as to what objectives are important to be achieved within an agreed-upon time period. An important facet of the joint session is linking the manager's objectives to the overall goals.
4. Measurement and control established so that supervisor-subordinate know when the objectives are achieved;
5. Review and recycle, the stage in which to evaluate the relative success of the subordinate in achieving the goals and to set new objectives for the next time period. The review and recycling usually take place once or twice each year.

The objectives should be measurable and specific; they should be described in output rather than input terms. For example, rather than say "Responsible for training new administrative assistants," the objective should be expressed as, "Will train five new administrative assistants to be fully functional by the end of the year." There are any number of ways to express objectives—units produced, costs cut, margins of profit, return on investment, sales increased, nature and amount of services delivered, safety record improved, etc.

Time is very important in the MBO programs. The objectives should be stated in such a way that time is of the essence. One may establish short-range goals—a year, say—and long-range objectives—three to five years. But the long-range objectives should not be fudged, either; they should be stated as specifically as are those for the year. Otherwise they are too hard to measure. Vague, general objectives are difficult to measure and do not motivate strongly.

Priorities should be tied in to the objectives. Obviously, not all of the objectives carry the same value. A manager would not be considered successful who spent 80 percent of the time on objectives that accounted for only 20 percent of the accountability.

Management by objectives seems so natural—people in organizations have been doing variations on it for years. Certainly, goal setting is widely recognized as an integral part of the manager's job. Then why do we keep hearing laments about the failure of MBO programs?

One important reason is that people and their behavior are simply not considered in many organizations. Establishing an MBO program is not just a matter of installing new procedures. Extensive changes in people's behavior are usually required. Certainly a reorientation of priorities is. In many organizations, efficiency—which is primarily activity—has been more valued than effectiveness, which is results. Furthermore, as alluded to earlier, people may feel that MBO, as job enrichment, is a management ploy to get more work out of them without rewarding them more (since extrinsic rewards are not necessarily tied in with achievement of objectives).

There are other reasons for the high failure rate of MBO's systematic goal-setting and the high motivation potential that can come with it:

- Lack of commitment, quite frequently starting at the

top. After initial enthusiasm, management turns its attention to something else.

• Poor follow-up. Managers sometimes seem to feel that once the mechanics of MBO are established, the program runs itself. Reviewing and recycling are done on a hit-or-miss basis. It has been estimated that it takes about five years of conscientious follow-up for an MBO program to take root.

• Objectives are dictated to employees by higher management. Little or no thought is given to whether the objectives mean anything to the employees, or whether they understand the significance of the factors to the overall operation. If employees are to be motivated to achieve objectives, they must have the feeling of "ownership," which is one of the reasons goals or objectives are jointly established.

• Poor coaching and assistance. Between the formal interviews, once or twice a year, the manager usually needs informal sessions with the next superior to determine what is needed, to achieve effectiveness. In the hustle and bustle these informal sessions are often postponed and then forgotten.

• Objectives may not be those for which managers can be held accountable. There is among many managers confusion between the terms *responsible* and *accountable.* A manager may be *responsible* for the production of 50,000 units, yet be dependent upon others in the organization to achieve that production—purchasing, engineering and maintenance, perhaps other departments involved in the processing. The manager who is dependent upon the cooperation of others cannot be held strictly *accountable* for all failures to produce the 50,000 units. That is why group goal-setting is a practice that is on the increase. Since not everyone can be responsible *and* accountable for the same things, it makes sense to get together the people who are involved in the accountability and ask them to set objectives for the whole group. Thus, each manager would have individual objectives and would participate in those set by the entire work group.

• Too mechanical and routine. If the objectives set are simply increases of what is already being done—"Next year, we'll put out 60,000 units instead of 50,000"—then, over a period of time, the program loses much of its excitement. George Odiorne, the educator and consultant who perhaps has been more influential in spreading the MBO message than anyone else, emphasizes the inclusion of problem-solving and innovation in management by objectives. Thus, a manager might consider, in setting objectives, the solution to a problem that has inhibited the effectiveness of the operation—for example, high, costly turnover of employees. The reduction of turnover by 20 percent could be an objective. A director of marketing could formulate an innovative objective that might increase substantially the distribution of his product without substantially changing his costs (new methods of transportation, sharing warehousing, etc.) Goal-setting should automatically include the routine or present functions, a problem to be solved, an innovation to be introduced.

• Unrealistic goals and time. A program can suffer when managers are permitted to set too many objectives, or when those objectives are too complex, or when the time period for their achievement is too short. Unrealistically high goals insure failure, and repetitive failures result in low morale, which makes people stop trying.

Management by objectives is *not* simple. It is, as many organizations have discovered, not a package program that can be neatly slipped into place without effort. It has many human implications that too often are ignored, to the detriment of the program. Nor is MBO just a matter of common sense, as some old-time managers like to think.

MBO is squarely in the middle of the action, totally on target in any evaluation of the behavioral sciences and their relevance for the organization of today. It can lead to the establishment of an effective intrinsic and extrinsic reward program. And it is based on the premises that are gaining acceptance among behavioral scientists and managers today:

- Human behavior is goal-oriented. People act for a reason, to achieve something that they consider important and good for them.
- An objective will have more motivational power if it is seen by the employee as useful to him or her.
- People tend to accept objectives more readily and completely if they have had a role in defining them.
- If achievement is to play a part in employees' motivation, they must know when it is taking place. For, them to know how they are doing, feedback on progress and accomplishment is essential.
- Employees value others' recognition of their achievement. The more significant those others, the more valued the recognition.

## Cognitive Dissonance

A subtle goal that motivates many people in conflict and decision-making situations is *closure,* for which a synonymous term is *completion.* People in a situation involving the choice between two or more options are in a state of conflict. It is natural to want to resolve the conflict. When the conflict is properly resolved, the decision-maker is in harmony. When the conflict has not been settled, when there is not closure, there is, according to Leon Festinger, a psychologist at Stanford University, *cognitive dissonance.*

The concept is very useful in understanding why decisions that seemed sensibly arrived at and subscribed to by the decision-makers become unglued and have to be made over. Festinger's theory can also shed light on why some people, after making a decision, continue to behave as if they are still making a choice.

Festinger explains that, in such situations, the decision has been made, but the conflict that existed during the decision-making process has not been resolved. There is still a dissonance in the person who has made the decision, as opposed to a harmony and oneness that should exist after a conflict has been settled. Let's look at an example. A purchasing agent has to decide among four suppliers' products. Prices are different. Product specifications vary, as do delivery times, although all of the products fit within an acceptable range of performance. The agent decides. But after placing the orders, he reviews all the data again. He still experiences reservations. Festinger believes that the amount of dissonance after a decision is related to the degree of conflict felt originally. The more difficulty a person experiences in making the decision, the more problems he or she may have in justifying the chosen course of action.

Thus, in trying to reduce the dissonance, the sense of irresolution, the decision-maker has to seek data that would reassure him or her that the decision was, after all, the proper one to make. An example is the person who, having put a deposit on a new car, continues to read the new car advertisements to bolster the rightness of the choice.

Festinger's research suggests to the manager who wants to reduce cognitive dissonance the need to: (1) take care to gather the needed relevant information so that one has sufficient data on which to make an educated choice, and (2) spend more time evaluating the options before the decision is made. These points are significant for a manager in understanding the motivations of people in conflict and decision-making situations.

## The Achievers

Harvard professor David C. McClelland's theories on achievement motivation emphasize that people can be helped to build such a motivation in themselves. McClelland's work began with his attempts to identify people who are motivated by the thought of achieving something. They do things rather than just think about them. The achievement-oriented person translates thought into action. The accomplishment, in McClelland's conviction, is often an end in itself. These are the salespeople-entrepreneur types. They want success and the feeling of achievement. They have a deep interest in their work. Money and other extrinsic rewards are appreciated, but it is really the successful completion of the work that holds the greatest motivational appeal.

Some people will work very hard for the money without having much interest in the kind of work done to get it. They go where the greatest opportunities are of making it. But for the achievement-oriented person, the extrinsic rewards are to be enjoyed and they do indicate success.

The following are indicators for McClelland's description of an achievement-motivated person:

• People with high *n* Achievement (*n* Ach) tend to set moderate goals for themselves and to work harder when the chances of succeeding are only moderate. They're not interested in attaining objectives that are easy to reach. At the same time, they avoid setting goals that there is only a slim chance of achieving. The goals should be realistic, yet challenging.

• The achievers prefer work situations in which they can take personal responsibility for the performance necessary to achieve their goals. For this reason the achiever will not gamble—gambling is chance. The person with high *n* Ach does not work easily in a committee or in collaboration with others, since some of the control over the work is in others' hands.

• High *n* Ach people like to get feedback as to how well they are doing and are responsive to that concrete feedback. The achiever is more likely to build a machine than to write a book. A machine works or it does not, gives a clear indication of success or a lack of it. A book, on the other hand, may not provide an undeniable success indicator. For example, the book may be read widely, but that may be due to promotion. Besides, the feedback takes too long.

• Achievement-motivated people are much more experimental. They like to try new things. They travel, move around, seek opportunity much more than people who do not have high *n* Ach. McClelland's term for this is *researching the environment.*

McClelland's conclusions for the manager who would like to help increase employees' motivations are these: People can be helped to set goals that involve moderate risks, risks that are reasonable and realistic given the person's ability level and resources; they need measurements to know how well they are doing, a feedback that comes automatically from progress as well as from others who are in a position to know; people like to have control over their work so they can take credit for it.

Another message from McClelland's work seems to be that people can learn to value intrinsic rewards—what flows from achievement—if they have the chance to attain them through some control over the efforts they are required to make, and if they have concrete evidence that they have succeeded in attaining those rewards.

Throughout this chapter, in all of the techniques described that are designed to increase motivation, these themes occur:

- Help people to set goals that reflect their values.
- Give them assistance in achieving those goals.
- Provide them with measurements of success.
- Reward them for achievement.

# Changing People's Behavior

Talking about changing people's behavior makes many people nervous. The more scientific term, *behavior modification,* seems to be even scarier. Both phrases apparently evoke connotations of brainwashing and personality molding. But the behavioral scientists—most of them, anyway—who talk about behavior modification are not referring to anything so sinister and dehumanizing. The way a person acts can be shaped in part by the foreseeable consequences of his voluntary, unbrainwashed actions. To use a homely example, a person at a party drinks too much. There are consequences, unpleasant ones. For one thing, the partygoer's body "punishes" the excess by providing headaches, nausea, nervousness, etc. Too, the excessive drinker learns that some of his friends at the party have expressed disapproval of the way he downed the martinis. Thus, the person realizes that the consequences of such actions will be painful. Next time, the realization of those consequences may encourage more moderate drinking practices. Behavior, in a small way, has been shaped.

Or there is positive influence—behavior that is rewarded tends to be reinforced and therefore is likely to be repeated.

There is much talk of reinforcement these days. People, it is assumed, do things for a reason that has value to them. When, as a result of a particular action, the person gets what is wanted, the chances are increased that he or she will repeat the action when he wants the same or similar consequences. The employee who values the esteem of the boss tries to behave in such a way as to please the superior. When the boss smiles and praises the good work of the subordinate, the latter feels reinforced or rewarded.

The psychological phrase that describes this process is *operant conditioning,* a term closely associated with Harvard professor B. F. Skinner. Although Skinner's research in conditioning processes was conducted largely with pigeons (an association that often brings about pejorative references to Skinner), reinforcement can be effective in modifying human behavior.

Positive reinforcement is one aspect of operant conditioning. Certain acts are rewarded. For example, a student is told by her teacher that there is an object in the classroom she wants the student to find. The teacher doesn't identify the object or its location, but she promises to drop a penny in a jar each time the student makes a step toward the object. The money collected will be turned over to the student once she has identified and touched the object. The student will begin to concentrate on taking steps that result in pennies dropped into the jar. First the general direction is discovered—away from the blackboard and windows, toward a bookshelf in the back of the room. Several books are touched with no sound of a coin. The hand moves tentatively toward a history book. A penny is dropped. The book is touched. Another penny.

The actions of the student have been shaped by the reinforcement provided by the pennies.

A careless typist who is unconcerned about typographical errors in his work can be encouraged, through reinforcement, to change his behavior to being concerned with error-free work. The reinforcement may be continuing praise or an increase in his weekly salary. Once the behavior has been shaped, it can be maintained through an intermittent schedule of reinforcement. To continue to say after each typing job, "Wow! This is perfect, as usual," will sound silly after a time. Or the typist won't hear it at all. But to say from time to time, "You continue to maintain your standard of excellence. We're very fortunate to have you here," or some such recognition will usually suffice in maintaining behavior.

Positive reinforcement is widely advocated today. To be effective, it should be given observing the following factors:

**Immediacy.** For best effects, reinforce as quickly after the act as possible so that it is clear precisely what is being reinforced.

**Specificity.** Make sure there is no doubt in the other person's mind as to what action is being recognized—so that it can be repeated.

**Proportion.** Make the recognition fit the achievement. Too much is phony, too little is easily forgotten.

**Consistency.** While shaping the desired behavior, continue to reinforce the behavior you want. Lapses and omissions confuse.

Reward the behavior you want; don't reward the behavior you don't want. That's the essential advice for those who would practice positive reinforcement. You want to discourage certain behavior in someone else. Be sure not to reinforce it. Anger over a bad habit can paradoxically reinforce. One salesman continually submitted his reports late; each time his manager bawled him out. But that, to the salesman, was reinforcement, for it was the only time his manager paid attention to him.

To withdraw reinforcement is to extinguish behavior. Another way to extinguish behavior is to punish: "I'll fire you if you don't stop coming in late."

Reinforcement is becoming a widely used management technique. It is most effective when it is nonmanipulative— that is, when the behavior desired is clearly defined and the reinforcements unmistakably point to the repetition of that behavior and no other. Reinforcement means something when it comes from a person who is respected. The reinforcement, whether it is money, praise, advancement, or whatever, should be something the subject likes and appreciates.

One major problem with positive reinforcement is that it is sometimes difficult to know what form of reinforcement will be effective. Too, there may be occasions when what is being reinforced can't be made precisely clear.

Kurt Lewin tackled some of these problems when he advanced his field theory: The study of a person depends upon the "field" that person is operating in—the environment, the circumstances, the factors operating upon the person. How can one determine the forces that are operating upon a person or an organization to change, and those that are militating against it? We shall examine a technique for such a determination in the next section.

## Force-Field Analysis

Psychologist Kurt Lewin stressed that organizations—and the people in them—tend to seek and maintain equilibrium. That is, for every pressure to effect change, there is a corresponding pressure to maintain conditions as they are. The person seeking change may increase the pressure, the "driving force," to bring change about. Unfortunately, people and conditions militating against the change will add sufficient pressure, the "restraining force," to offset that increased pressure from the so-called change agent. Figure 1 illustrates the present—equilibrium.

# DRIVING          RESTRAINING

# NOW

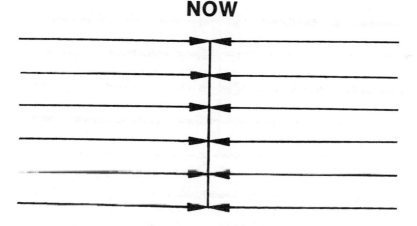

*Fig. 1. Equilibrium: opposing forces are in balance.*

The arrows on both sides of the center line, representing conditions as they exist at present, are of equal intensity. If one of the driving forces is increased, one or more restraining forces will grow in intensity to offset it, as shown in figure 2.

Identifying the drivers and restrainers is part of Force-Field Analysis (FFA), an approach—developed from Lewin's thought—for analyzing a situation and for devising specific steps to alter it. There are three possible ways of overcoming equilibrium and thus creating change:

1. *Add* a new force or forces.
2. *Delete* an old force or forces.
3. *Alter* the magnitude of forces—increase the driver(s) and/or decrease the restrainer(s).

# DRIVING                    RESTRAINING

## NOW

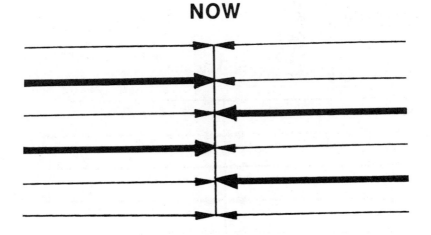

*Fig. 2. Disequilibrium.*

FFA can be used to point to changes that can be made in individuals and organizations. Take an organization as an example: A high-level executive wishes to decrease the number of secretaries in the organization and create, instead, a service group known as a *word-processing center* (WPC). Typists in the center would take over the stenographic and routine typing duties of the secretaries, freeing the latter to do more sophisticated and higher-level duties. In arguing for the change, this executive is actually naming what Lewin would call driving forces. Some of them, in this example, would be:

• *Efficient scheduling.* Presently some secretaries appear to be overloaded while others are not. Or they have work peaks and valleys. In a WPC, a supervisor could assign organizational work to even out peaks and valleys.

• *Lower costs.* Letters and other typed material can be produced at less cost by using better scheduling and lower salaries of typists. Also, less equipment may be needed for the center than for each executive or supervisor.

• *Sophisticated equipment.* Production of letters, memos, and reports can be accomplished through sophisticated, automated equipment which the use of a WPC can justify.

• *Utilization of resources.* Some secretaries prefer typing and more routine functions to varied secretarial duties. They can be assigned to the WPC. Those who want higher-level and supervisory work are freed to prepare themselves for such advancement.

The above are some of the major driving forces. There are undoubtedly others, such as consistency of quality and more efficient utilization of space, for example.

But there are also restraining forces. Both executives and secretaries may see a loss of status. The former also fear the work will be less competent if it is done outside their direct control. Everyone worries about the impersonality of the arrangement. There could be increased delays in getting the work out.

Figure 3 illustrates the major drivers and restrainers as the executive may see them.

The executive considers which of the driving forces can be increased. He or she displays to peers and subordinates the attractiveness of the new equipment and demonstrates its efficiency on a project involving the sending of personal, individually typed letters to two hundred major customers. The shorter time required to complete the job, and the consistent quality of the letters, are telling arguments.

Another significant driving force is in the reassignment of secretaries. Executives are advised that those secretaries capable of moving up to increased responsibilities will reflect favorably upon the bosses with whom they had been associated—in short, a new evaluation area has been

## DRIVERS                              RESTRAINERS

## NOW

| DRIVERS | RESTRAINERS |
|---|---|
| Efficient scheduling | Fear of loss of status |
| Lower costs | Less-competent work |
| Sophisticated equipment | Delays |
| Utilization of resources | Impersonality |
| Quality | Loss of one-to-one control |

*Fig. 3. Drivers and restrainers influencing one executive's WPC decision.*

created to make some executives look better and get better appraisals than before.

But it is also necessary for the executive to reduce as many of the restraining forces as he can. He asks himself:

- Which restraining forces can be altered quickly with little effort and cost?
- Which restraining forces, if altered, are likely to have the greatest impact?
- Which restraining forces can be altered with the least disruption?

The feeling of regimentation, at least among the secretaries and stenographers reassigned to the WPC, can be
alleviated by permitting them some choice as to the hours
they work. It may also be possible to give the members of
the WPC some latitude in selecting the kinds of work they
can specialize in. The flexible hours, incidentally, offer a
distinct benefit to the executive who, at five minutes before
five, realizes he must get out a letter or a memo for the
following morning. Before, he would have had to wait until
the next day or ask a secretary to work overtime. Now he
can be assured of having his work done by someone who is
working after five in the WPC.

The impersonality is harder to deal with, but it can be
lessened by having short seminars in which the members
of the WPC work with executives to improve communication
and dictating skills between them. Of much more impact for
some of the secretaries is the potential for greater respon-
siblity, either as supervisors in the WPC or as administrative
managers for groups of executives.

Force-Field Analysis can be used on short- as well as
long-range problems, decisions, projects, and plans. It is
useful in pointing the ways to modify behavior as well as
bring change to organizations. Its primary value lies in the
way it helps make visible more factors and options; it also
helps in identifying the specific driving and restraining
forces. Once these factors are identified, a person can see
how to make those adjustments in the force field that will
help achieve change in the most constructive way. The
significant point is that in the case of personal change,
the environmental or organizational conditions must be
considered.

In Lewin's approach, the change would occur if the
positive factors or rewards prevail. On the other hand, if
negative factors increase to meet the stronger force of the
positive, the restrainers—restraining the person from

changing—are still dominant, and the inferior "now" condition—the status quo—continues.

## Gestalt

No discussion of behavior change would be complete without mentioning *Gestalt* therapy. The German word *Gestalt* means "entirety," "the whole," a concept that every manager has been exposed to recently with respect to employees: dealing with the whole person. The Gestalt therapy movement, if that's what it can be called properly, resembles Transactional Analysis in some ways. In fact, some TA practitioners are very Gestalt in their perspective and practice. Both movements, incidentally, were born on the West Coast of the United States. Both received their greatest impetus from psychoanalysts who broke with the Freudian perspective. Both were conceived of as therapies.

Gestalt therapy is credited to Fritz Perls, who taught workshops at Esalen for several years. Psychoanalysis is thought of as treatment of deviation from mental health, whether the deviation be a neurosis or a psychosis. Gestalt therapy, on the other hand, deals not so much with human *illness* as with human *potential.* Perls refers to holes in the personality, holes to be filled.

Gestalt is also a reaction to the Puritanical tradition to which many Americans are subject—division into absolutes: black and white, good and bad, etc.—and especially the distinction between what we are and what we have. For example, most people talk about their bodies and organs in terms of possession—my body, my mind, I have a liver, etc.

In Gestalt we would view our parts as ourselves. The emphasis is on completeness, wholeness. Perls advocates control of the organism by the organism itself, which is why he terms Gestalt an existential perspective—each organism is complete and unique. Each healthy, whole, complete organism determines its fate, conduct, behavior, etc.

Perls credits Freud with the discovery of the *superego,* which in Gestalt therapy is called the *top dog*, the idealist, the perfectionist in people, constantly dictating *shoulds* to the person, who is really the underdog, at the mercy of the top dog. The person is forever struggling to live up to the ideals and perfectionism of the top dog, which has probably been programmed by others (see the analogy to TA and the Parent). As a result, says Perls, we live patterned behavior—our responses to what happens to us are programmed and determined in advance. We both play roles and make responses that are predictable and categorized, when, in Perls's view, only two things should control us: the environment and our own nature. Put another way, the here and now are the essentials, in Perls's outlook. What I do should be determined not by what others have insisted on teaching me to do, but by the present situation and my present state of being. Our response to what is going on now is most important. The past is an unfinished situation, and the cause of much of our problems, for we are probably still trying to deal with unfinished business. The future is an expectation for which we try to rehearse. Therefore our response to the future is patterned not according to what actually happens but by what we think will happen.

According to Perls, we mature by moving from being environmentally supported to being self-supported. The analogy he was fond of using was that of the baby who, accustomed to breathing and getting its blood supply and nutrients through the umbilical cord, now—having been born—must breathe on its own, use its own independent blood system. However, death would occur if the baby had to discard its former survival system but was unable to develop one of its own. This is, in Gestalt, true of the psychological: People sometimes cannot let go of the support systems they have been relying on from the outside, from the past, from tradition, from others. They reach an impasse, get stuck, cannot make the transition to being self-supporting.

One of the means of help advocated by Perls in such a situation is a potentially interesting useful tool for the manager: the empty chair. In Perls's work it was often referred to as the *hot* seat. The person occupying the hot seat might begin by describing a dream, a fantasy, or a problem. Whatever, the person is encouraged to talk. The dialogue takes place with an empty chair. Very often, it is felt in Gestalt therapy, people will apply to things or other creatures characteristics they would really like to apply to themselves. Consequently in the context of Gestalt it makes sense for the person to talk to this object or other creature, since it probably means he or she is addressing some aspect of himself. The person takes turns, first in this chair, then in that one, exchanging roles. Often the person addresses himself or herself to that which prevents the wholeness—a blockage, an inhibition. The main thing is the recognition that it exists.

The primary theme of Gestalt—the wholeness, the completeness of the person—has special relevance to the research of today when we are trying to establish the identity of the executive as a whole person.

Gestalt is discussed with greater frequency these days as an approach to helping people become more effective. It enables people in new problem-solving and decision-making situations to better evaluate surrounding circumstances and thus develop options that take into account the uniqueness of the situation. It has undeniable value in encouraging people to accept their totality, not just the parts and characteristics they think others will accept. The emphasis on self-support (rather than environmental support) and the here-and-now can point managers in the direction of freeing themselves from the traditional, organizational and self-imposed constraints and role-playing that inhibit growth.

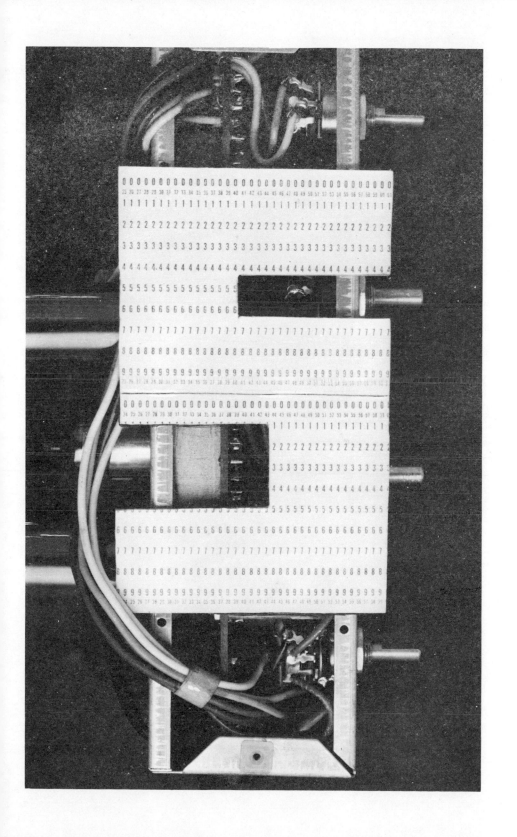

# What Goes On Between People

It is safe to suggest that nearly everyone wishes to be effective in dealing with others. That is, they want something good to come from their transactions. They want something from the other person—help, respect, friendship, affection, obedience, etc. Even in conflict, the disputants are looking for something to come out of their anger or debate—a sense of having won, the satisfaction of having demolished another person.

But it is also safe to say that many people are not always sure what they want from the transaction—or perhaps more correctly, they have an idea of what they want, but their behavior isn't consistent with that idea. Interpersonal competence, therefore, is increasingly recognized as a serious field for study.

## Transactional Analysis

Within the last decade we have seen an attempt to develop a system that would explain what goes on between people when they interact. This system is called transactional analysis (TA). Not only does it try to illuminate; it also purports to help people understand what others are communicating and to develop appropriate and constructive responses to those communications.

Probably no other attempt to formularize how people relate to one another has so captured the fancy of people as TA, which is the brainchild of the late psychiatrist Eric Berne. Berne, it will be remembered, wrote the best-selling book *Games People Play* in the 1960s. In the beginning, Transactional Analysis was the foundation of a therapy. But it has moved far beyond the analyst's office. In a more simplified and universal form, it has been introduced into hundreds of organizations to teach people how to be more effective when they deal with each other.

One reason for the immense popularity of TA, proponents say, is that it *works*. People trained in TA often report they can handle their transactions with others in a more satisfying manner. Furthermore, Transactional Analysis is relatively easy to teach to people who otherwise have no extensive knowledge of psychology. It may seem oversimplified, a bit too "packaged," but there is no question that multitudes are convinced that it can help them become more mature, more effective in their relationships.

The foundations of TA are three ego states: Parent, Adult, Child. All three are legitimate and natural to the person, and people shift from one ego state to another in their transactions.

The Parent ego state is one in which we act upon transmitted knowledge, usually from our parents, but from other sources as well. The Parent can be *nurturing:* "Go ahead and cry, it will be good for you to get it all out." The Parent is also *critical:* "If you would listen to me, you wouldn't get into these messes." There's a *prejudicing* side of the parent also: "Decent women don't go into bars alone."

There are certain words and phrases that are familiar to the Parent ego state. On the positive or nurturing side:

There, there;

It will turn out all right, you'll see;

You can do it;

That was a good job.

The critical, negative, prejudicial Parent resorts to such words and phrases as:

I told you;

You should;

You must;

You mustn't;

Why didn't you . . .

The Child ego state is impulsive, enthusiastic, curious, experimental. Just as the infant responds spontaneously and naturally to impulses and stimuli, naturalness and spontaneity characterize the Child ego state (childlike as well as childish). Just as the Parent ego state can have different aspects, the Child can be:

• *The Natural Child*—the untrained infant, exploring, showing pleasure, sensuous, affectionate, uncensored. But the Natural Child is also self-indulgent, self-centered, rebellious, fearful.

• *The Little Professor*—intuitive, creative, and manipulative. The Little Professor, although but a child, catches messages in other people's tone of voice, expression, or other nonverbal communications. The Creative Child throws off constraints to come up with a different design or plan, builds things, fantasizes. But the Creative Child is also manipulative, currying favor or drawing sympathy to get his or her way.

• *The Adapted Child*—responsive to outside authority and to interactions with the environment. The Adapted Child ("Adapted" because he has learned to adapt) learns to comply, even though grudgingly, to the demands of authority. Withdrawal is another way this child responds to authority or environment. Another characteristic is procrastination, a behavior chosen when the child doesn't wish to comply and doesn't dare to rebel.

Some commonly used expressions in the Child state, under positive and negative connotations:

| Positive | Negative |
|----------|----------|
| I feel good; | I want it; |
| This is great; | I can't; |
| I like you; | Yes, but; |
| You're nice. | I don't feel like it. |

The Adult ego state is not a reflection of a person's age. The Adult is acting when the person reasons, gathers facts, tries to be objective, processes data. The Adult develops options, chooses the one that seems most realistic in the situation. Anticipating the consequences of an action or decision is characteristic of this ego state. Some commonly heard Adult words and phrases:

> Let's think about this.
> What are the facts?
> What do you think?
> Let's do some planning.
> Shall we talk about it?

No one ego state is, of itself, superior to the others. The effective person needs all three to function. A person who never acts spontaneously or impulsively, who doesn't now and then entertain fantasies or indulge in wishful thinking, who can't admit—and lament over—frustration or disappointment, who is unable to operate on his or her own apart from parental counsel and direction, can hardly be an interesting person. Worse, such a person would be incomplete, narrow, even emotionally crippled.

The complaint is often expressed that the Child ego state is honored in theory but suppressed in practice. Even some

TA practitioners admit that they spend less time in training programs with this ego state than with the other two. Certainly the atmosphere in many organizations seems to militate against acting from the Child state—that is, being openly emotional, impulsive, affectionate, nonrational.

But all three ego states are needed and desirable. However, what is most desirable, according to many TA proponents, is for the Adult to act as "executive" for all three. When such is the case, they explain, the data received are examined by the Adult, who then determines what kind of response from which ego state is appropriate. The Adult also evaluates the recorded information as to validity and examines the Child to see whether the feelings there are suitable for the present. Data and feelings that are invalid and inappropriate are discarded. It is safe to say that the above description of the Adult as executive is an ideal, a hoped-for condition. The Adult state is itself continually influenced and reshaped by education and experience.

## Transactions

When a person communicates with another, he or she expects a message of response. These two-part communications are called *transactions,* which TA classifies as complementary, crossed, or ulterior.

In a complementary transaction the response expected from the other person is actually given:

1. I'm so rushed to finish this report I can't even think. (An appeal to the Parent for sympathy and understanding.)
2. Don't let yourself get so upset. Why don't I extend your deadline until tomorrow to take the pressure off.

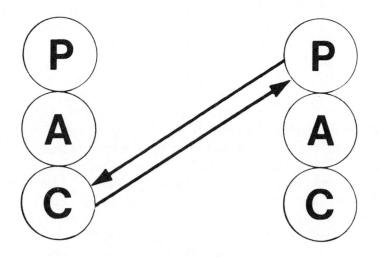

*Fig. 4. Diagram of a complementary transaction.*

The above was an example of a Child/Nurturing Parent transaction (figure 4). It could easily have been a *crossed*

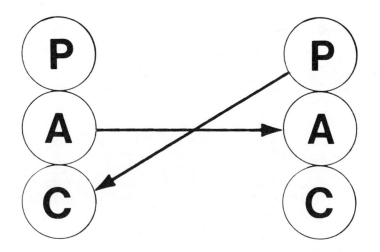

*Fig. 5. Diagram of a crossed transaction.*

*transaction,* which occurs when an *unexpected* response is made. To illustrate:

1. I'm running out of time to finish this report.
2. If you hadn't waited so long to start it, you wouldn't have to rush.

The first statement was a realization that the report would not be finished by the deadline. The response was by a Critical Parent to a "procrastinating" Child (figure 5).

Another example of a complementary transaction:

1. What time is it?
2. Three-thirty.

A straight transaction, obviously Adult-Adult (figure 6). But instead, suppose the response is, "Is something wrong?" The first person then may say, "Why do you always make such a big deal, I just wanted to know the time."

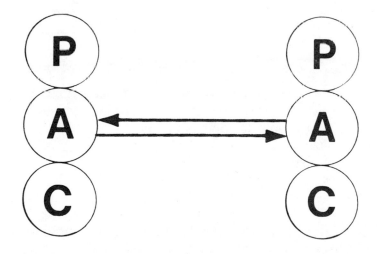

*Fig. 6. Diagram of a complementary transaction (compare with fig. 4).*

That rejoinder—an Adult asking a question, a Child complaining to a suspicious Parent—probably finishes the exchange, which is what often happens in a crossed transaction (figure 7). Everything stops—or goes in another direction. In a complementary transaction (see figure 6), the lines of communication remain open for further exchanges.

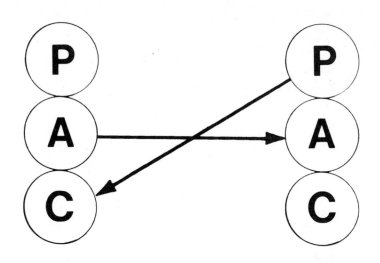

*Fig. 7.  A crossed transaction (compare with fig. 5).*

Of course, words are only one indicator of the kind of transaction: gestures, facial expression, posture, and tone of voice all contribute to identifying the transaction as one kind or other.

For example:

Husband: "I feel so bad. My head is killing me."

Wife: "I'm sorry to hear that. Let me get you some aspirin."

But suppose, instead of offering sympathy and aspirin, the wife responded like a critical Parent (figure 8):

"Don't expect sympathy from me. I told you not to play golf in the rain yesterday."

The conversation may not stop there, although com-

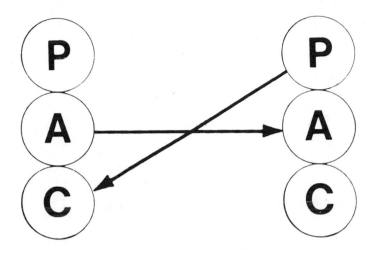

*Fig. 8. A crossed transaction.*

munication probably will. The transaction may take a querulous, argumentative turn. In that case, another transaction might help after each has thrown harsh words at the other (figure 9):

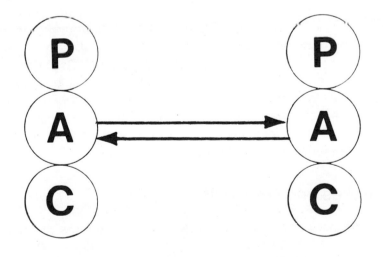

*Fig. 9. A complementary transaction.*

Husband: "Do you feel as silly as I do, arguing this way?"
Wife: "Yes; it is foolish, isn't it?"

An *ulterior transaction* (figure 10) involves more than one ego state, or more than one aspect of the same state. A

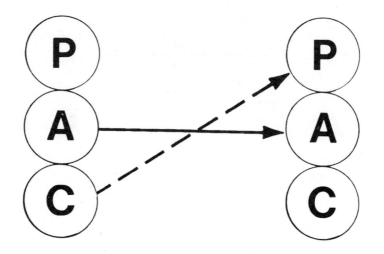

*Fig. 10. An ulterior transaction.*

covert message is sent disguised as a socially acceptable transaction. In their book *Born to Win*, Muriel James and Dorothy Jongeward cite the example of the alcoholic who comes to work with a hangover and boasts, "Boy, I really blew it last night and drank myself under the table. What a head I've got today!" The message seems straight. However, as James and Jongeward observe, "The alcoholic's Child ego state is looking for the Parent in the other to smile indulgently and thus condone his drinking."

## Strokes and Discounts

"Everyone needs strokes." That is a central tenet of TA. A stroke is a basic recognition (a reinforcement!) of another's existence. There are positive strokes—smiling, giving a compliment on someone's work, praising, expressing affection and respect, etc.—and there are negative strokes—gossiping, finding fault, ignoring, sarcasm, interrupting, condescending or contemptuous looks, harsh criticism, humiliation. Positive strokes are sometimes referred to as "warm fuzzies"—negative strokes as "cold pricklies."

So needed are strokes, TA maintains, that a person deprived of positive strokes will seek negative ones. The salesman who never has constructive contact with his manager and consistently sends his reports in late is begging for a call and a bawling-out from the boss. It is negative stroking, but the only kind the salesman feels he can get.

*Discounting* is a form of negative stroking. To illustrate, one person in a group makes a suggestion. Immediately, another person speaks up to make a different suggestion without acknowledging the colleague, who then feels "discounted." Another form of discounting is denial of another person's feelings. The first person says, "I'm feeling very anxious." A second speaks up, "Nonsense!" The first person's feelings have been discounted.

Essentially, any time the message, "You're not important," is conveyed, it's a discount.

## Permissions, Scripts, and Life Positions

During a TA workshop the author attended, the leader passed around crayons and large sheets of drawing paper. She asked the participants to draw a picture of the nonhuman, living thing for which each of them had the greatest affection. Some participants portrayed cats, dogs, horses, flowers, birds, etc. Then they were asked to write down eight or ten characteristics of the thing they had drawn. Samples: courageous, lovable, cuddly, cute, affectionate, loyal, trustworthy, lovely. Each participant read aloud the characteristics, "He (she, or it) is . . ."

Finally they were asked to read off the adjectives once more, this time prefixing the characteristic with "I am . . ." It was a startling experience for most. It was not easy, for example, for a six-foot-tall man weighing 200 pounds to say, "I am cuddly; I am cute." But when asked by others whether he could "own" the statements, he admitted that he had on a number of occasions been encouraged to think of himself in those terms by certain women he had associated with (and had secretly allowed himself to visualize himself those ways).

The point of the exercise was this: One's Parent censors what otherwise the Child would think of oneself. Since, by conditioning and upbringing, we are not permitted to think of ourselves in terms that compliment, we ascribe the characteristics we have censored about ourselves to other creatures. To own those descriptive terms, we must give ourselves permission. This is an illustration of the understanding of and respect for the Child ego state in Transactional Analysis. As the workshop leader put it, "The Child is ageless."

Another constraint that Transactional Analysis explains is scripting, a life plan that an individual feels compelled to play out. He or she may not be very aware of the "script"— another term fo conditioning—but it has been "written" in the transactions the individual has had with parents and others. People learn to play roles and often seek others to play complementary roles. An individual script is exemplified by the young man who told his therapist he had problems mixing socially, because he had always been told by his mother that he was the shy thinker, whereas his brother had the personality and was liked by everyone (with the implication that the thinker would have problems getting people to like him).

Not only individuals follow scripting. Families, organizations, cultures, and nations also are scripted. An example of a family script: "The Franklin women have always done their grieving in private." Organizations may try to define how employees should perceive themselves, dictating conduct, appearance, attitudes. As for national scripting: an extreme example is Nazi Germany.

As a result of scripting, a person holds a life position, of which there are four:

1. "I'm OK, you're OK." This position is considered mentally healthy. The person in this life position is realistic, has valid expectations (they prove not to be too low or too high), and accepts people without great difficulty.

2. "I'm OK, you're not OK." People who see themselves and others thus probably feel put upon or down by others, persecuted. Paranoia may develop from such a position, and then aggressive behavior to match.

3. "I'm not OK, you're OK." The people in this position feel powerless. When they compare themselves to others, they come out on the short end. Withdrawal, depression, even suicide sometimes follow.

4. "I'm not OK, you're not OK." This is a radically antisocial position, often leading to schizoid behavior, suicide, or even homicide.

TA has been criticized—at times justifiably—for reducing so many complexities to simple formulations. In recent years the body of knowledge constituting TA has grown tremendously in an effort to encompass the phenomena people experience in life. More elaborate and specific games and transactions are showing up in the literature. Still, because of its all-encompassing approach, it is increasingly popular with individuals and organizations alike.

## Competition

Competition, traditionally revered for its role in free enterprise, characterizes many interactions. But, as Harvard professor and author Chris Argyris points out, people in organizations invest tremendous amounts of energy in competing with one another, with disproportionately little output for the benefit of the organization. One well-known psychologist, Robert B. Morton, puts participants in his Organization Development Laboratory through a competitive exercise that shows vividly what an energy drain it can be. In a typical lab, there might be two groups. Each group appoints a judge; the judges render a decision as to which group does better work.

The assignment might involve each group's writing about some topic. The judges retire from the groups to develop their criteria—conciseness, logic, style, etc.—for deciding the best effort. (It is not unknown for participants to get so caught up in the effort that they are quite willing to work through the night to have a better composition than the other group can produce.) After the compositions are turned in to the judges, there is a general session in which the two groups come together to have their efforts judged (although they are unaware that the decision has already been made privately by the judges). A list of characteristics, positive and negative, describing the participants' perceptions of the characteristics the judges will bring to the decision-making—fair, open-minded, easily influenced, etc.—is filled out by each member of both groups. One spokesman from each group is appointed to sit at a table in the front of the room to "defend" the efforts of his or her own group and to make the other's product look bad in the eyes of the judge.

The debate often starts out as mannered and quiet. But as one representative makes a point against the other, there are groans and promptings. Notes are passed from each group to its representative to provide fresh ammunition. Soon it is easily apparent that each group is so caught up in the partisan activity that there is in fact no debate. It becomes a free-for-all, or, at the very least, the representatives end up conducting two monologues.

At the conclusion of the time allotted to the exchange, the

judges announce their decision. The list of characteristics of the judges, as perceived by the participants, is passed out again. Almost predictably, the winning group sees an increase in the number of positive attributes of the judges, who are perceived as even more honest and fair-minded and intelligent than before. In the losing group, the number of negative perceptions of the judges increases noticeably. There is little doubt, evidently, in the minds of the participants—or some of them—that the judges lack integrity, intelligence, etc. Otherwise how could the splendid efforts of the losing group have failed?

Only then do the judges reveal they had made their decision before the debate. The before-and-after lists of perceptions of the two groups are compared, and the sharp differences in them are noted and discussed. Often the group members' anger at having been manipulated is outweighed by their astonishment at how seriously and easily their perceptions have been distorted by the single-minded desire to win. Whatever strong feelings they have at the conclusion of the exercise are amplified as the participants recall similar, but real, competitive compulsions or obsessions in their organizations. The partisanship and rivalry that competition in organizations produces often will lead to serious polarization and conflict.

## Organizational Conflict

This same win-lose orientation exhibited in Morton's laboratory all too frequently characterizes the conflicts we see in our organizations. One party must win, the other lose. It is an either-or proposition. Unfortunately, the participants in organizational conflict seldom see clearly, even in retrospect, how distorted their perceptions have become, how the idea of winning can obsess them—possibly to the detriment of the overall organization.

How people in an organization view conflict is very important to the effectiveness of that organization. Social
psychology maintains that conflict is inevitable, although in
some traditional organizational cultures infighting is pub-
licly discouraged and decried. But so long as there are
people trying to advance their ideas and obtain support for
their projects, so long as the boundaries of authority and
responsibility are less than absolutely clear to everyone, so
long as John's perception of his job differs from Jill's opinion of what John should be doing, so long as you find
people in organizations ambitious for the power to do
things their way, so long as there are successes and failures, there will be conflict.

When the official policy is that conflict is to be avoided,
*overt* signs of fighting and disagreement are often absent.
In fact, members of the organization may have a standard
policy of withdrawing from even the recognition of problems and disagreements. In such a climate, problems don't
get confronted and solved.

But the covert behavior within the organization will be
pernicious. Between groups and departments there will be
withholding of information, or even supplying of misinforma-
tion; there will be favoritism (those who are on our side get
the best service and treatment); obstruction of procedures;
refusal to cooperate; no direct communication between
certain people and groups; duplication of efforts primarily
because this group will not accept that group's work methods; decisions will be made by one group without consultation with other groups affected; etc. Where people and
groups are in conflict, meetings are frequently characterized by cautious behavior—words are weighed, discussion is circumspect, and there are lots of hidden and personal agendas.

Basically, there are three approaches to the resolution of
conflicts in organizations: win-lose, lose-lose, and win-win.
In **win-lose**, there is often the recognition by both dispu-

tants or conflicting groups (interpersonal conflict usually becomes intergroup in nature very quickly if the personalities have any status at all—otherwise the conflict is probably not worth thinking about) that whatever the resolution, one side will take all, or close to it. This recognition often means a prolongation—and escalation—of the conflict until one group thinks it can take the spoils. (It may also mean an avoidance of important issues underlying the conflict if the chances of winning are not clear to either disputant.)

The usual win-lose resolution is accomplished in one of two ways: either one side eventually becomes more powerful than the other in some way, or there is an appeal to higher authority. In the former, one side may gain in credibility or authority, or, when engaged in competition, point to successful achievement and thereby gain more influence "at court."

In appealing to a higher authority, a great deal of maneuvering and politicking must sometimes go on to influence the authority, who then makes a judgment that too often reflects an either-or deliberation—this way or that, this group or that.

In the win-lose conflict resolution, decision or result is usually imposed on the loser. And it is seldom accepted graciously.

An imposed compromise sometimes takes place in the **lose-lose** approach. Or the groups are under pressure to bargain and to arrive at a compromise. Very often the result is that neither group gets what it wants, nor can either group view the outcome as a win. Probably the resentment will continue, and the conflict will reappear.

Using the knowledge and tools the behavioral sciences provide, organizations today have three generally successful ways of creating **win-win** resolutions: changing rewards, altering perceptions, and developing goals.

**Changing rewards.** Unfortunately, the rewards in many

organizations are geared to promoting competition between people, departments, and functions. The competitors get so caught up in trying to outdo everyone else
that they even try to defeat the organization. However, aggressive competitors get attention.

Their aggressiveness may seem to them the only way to
try to get what they want. To offset this, management must
offer rewards based on achievement of overall organizational goals; provide opportunities for collaboration (joint
projects, task forces and interfunctional or interdepartmental activity); encourage group goal-setting in which successful achievement depends upon collaboration.

Initiating ideas, fostering horizontal communications between peers and departments, openly confronting issues
that are the bases of conflict: These are also activities that
should be rewarded.

**Altering perceptions.** In the event of conflict between,
say, two groups, a number of techniques can be used to
take the prejudice and extreme subjectivity out of the disputants' perceptions of the issues, the behavior of the other
party, and their own actions. Some frequently used methods, following initial separation of the conflicting groups,
are:

- Ask the separate groups to write down how they see
  the issues or the problems. Also ask them to list the
  factors that have contributed to making the problem
  what it is. The second list usually points the collective finger at the other group and the contributions
  they have made toward the growth of the problem.
- A variation on the above is to suggest that each
  group also try to list what it believes the other group
  will list as contributing factors. This approach starts
  each group looking at itself, providing some basis
  for positive discussion when the groups come together with their respective data.

- Each group writes down how it sees the other group's behavior. Then a second list is drawn up speculating how the other group may see itself. Each group draws up a third list that details how it believes itself viewed by the absent group. Again, some of the behaviors exacerbating the conflict get put on paper to provide common areas of discussion and comparison when the two groups meet.

The data generated in any of the above approaches can be first exchanged in writing or else introduced directly into the meeting between the groups. The important first step is to get each group to acknowledge that the other has its perceptions of the conflict that are in variance with its own.

**Developing goals.** A third approach to resolving conflict on a win-win basis is to substitute goals for problems. Instead of asking such questions as who is to blame, who has done the most to create this, how can we correct the deviation, etc., pose the issue this way: What would we prefer as an alternative to the present situation? Seeking an alternative, or options, tends to take the conversation away from the causes of the problem, away from who is to blame (from which point it may go no further).

Once an alternative has been fairly well defined, then the questions can be asked: What are we not doing now that we need to do in order to achieve this alternative? What are we doing now that gets in the way of reaching our goal? Who is responsible for seeing that we develop the alternative? How is the responsibility to be distributed? By what date or in what time period shall this goal be achieved?

The advantage of setting goals rather than discussing problems is that instead of a patch-up job over problems, the discussion opens up opportunities for innovation. Resolving the conflict may yield completely new results. Whatever the approaches used to resolve conflict, it would

seem to be a rather radical notion in many organizations—
but perfectly compatible with the findings of the behavioral
sciences—that conflict is legitimate, even inevitable, if
things are to get done.

Within the past thirty years there have been attempts—as
we shall see—to train people to resolve conflicts by placing
them in groups where their behavior can be observed and
where they can take actions that will get immediate feedback and reinforcement, which are valuable contributors in
developing more effective behavior.

# People in Groups

Although people have been assigned to work in groups, teams, and departments for as long as there have been formal organizations, the thought of a work group as an entity, a body that exists with an identity, has not until recently really been taken seriously on a wide scale. As has been discussed, the informal group was observed as long ago as the Hawthorne studies, nearly fifty years ago. Some research in group dynamics—the behavior and interactions of people in small groups—was done during the 1930s and 1940s by Kurt Lewin, who felt that people's behaviors were actually influenced by the environment and the groups they were part of. But the idea of actually using groups to train people to be more effective in working with others had few adherents until the development of sensitivity training in the late 1940s.

## Sensitivity Training

There are those who believe that the development of sensitivity training is one of the more significant events in the history of psychology in this century. Probably few social psychologists would disagree, if our definition of "event" were to include the impetus given scientific study of the behavior of people in groups—the consequence of the T-group (T for training), an essential unit in sensitivity training.

Sensitivity training as we know it was a happy accident. Lewin, who had initiated and conducted extensive research in group behavior during the 1930s and 1940s, was a prime mover. In Lewin's view, behavior in a group is the product of the interaction between the individual and the social situation. The group is capable of modifying an individual member's behavior, enhancing or detracting from that person's effectiveness in dealing with others. Everyone has observed meetings or other group situations in which certain people seemed to perform exceptionally well—they did the right things, said the right things, won the cooperation and respect of others. Other individuals, who might be very skilled in one-to-one relationships, seem hampered in a group, creating for themselves and others obstacles to getting the job done. Still others perform well in one group setting and not another.

Lewin also felt that a group is an organism, an entity, not just an aggregate of individuals. There is such a thing, following his line of thought, as a group personality that can exist apart from the personalities of the members or even of the dominant members or leaders.

In the summer of 1946, Lewin and his associates were asked to conduct a leadership training program for the Connecticut State Inter-Racial Commission. The objective of the program was to help community representatives develop greater skills in dealing with other people. Each evening, after the sessions had concluded for the day, Lewin and his staff met to evaluate the results of the day's work and to discuss the behavior of the trainees in the groups.

One evening, a few of the trainees asked to sit in on the evaluation session, and Lewin agreed. The feedback they received on their behavior stimulated them to talk about their own perceptions of what they had done and why. Lewin became quite enthusiastic about the new kinds of data that were being generated. For the remaining evenings of the session, the other participants sat in, providing similar perceptions and feedback.

Kurt Lewin died that winter, but the revolutionary idea of using training groups did not. An organization, National Training Laboratories (NTL), was formed to advance the new learning technique—soon to be called Sensitivity Training. In the summer of 1947, NTL held its first T-groups on the campus of a boys' school in Bethel, Maine. Not quite thirty years later, NTL, based near Washington, D.C., still conducts sensitivity training sessions around the country, and it also offers more specialized programs for various professionals.

The basic structure of sensitivity training is the T-group, averaging perhaps eight to twelve people. There are three aspects of group activity. At a meeting, there is usually a formal agenda: a problem, or a decision to be made, or perhaps a project to be designed. In group-dynamics terms, this is referred to as *content*, the matter to be discussed.

How the content is to be discussed and dealt with is the *method*. What is the form of leadership? Is everyone to be allowed to speak on the subject? Are time limits to be imposed, or a maximum number of meetings? Is the decision to be arrived at by consensus, or by a simple majority? Are parliamentary rules to be observed? What powers are to be given the chair?

Sensitivity training is less highly structured than most learning. The group participants themselves generally determine how they spend their time. There is usually a facilitator, not infrequently referred to as a group leader.

The facilitator is often a practicing or teaching psychologist with an advanced degree. And the role of the facilitator is just that—to facilitate the learning and the group *process*.

*Process* has to do with the interactions between people—their behavior with each other. Behavior in a group setting can be *con*structive, or it can be *ob*structive. Participants in a meeting can encourage one another to speak out on the issues; they can support efforts to introduce ideas; they can focus on the objectives of the group in their deliberations. On the other hand, people can engage in feuds that have little or nothing to do with the issues the group is trying to deal with; one or more members can succeed in dominating the meeting to push through partisan projects, to gain personal ends; people can use the meeting as an arena or showcase for their own abilities to the extent that others give up trying to achieve group objectives.

These interactions—sometimes subtle, subversive, enhancing, destructive, supportive—should be recognized so that those behaviors that contribute to making the group more effective in reaching its goals can be encouraged and repeated. Too, those actions and words that get in the way of the goals, that lead the group off the track, can be corrected and discouraged. In "processing," which is the reporting of process, people observe what is going on between participants and describe it to others, as well as to the people involved in the interactions. Giving feedback, and leveling, are part of the processing.

Some examples of feedback are these:

• "You keep interrupting me when I'm trying to say something, and I feel as if I'm being cut off. I wish you wouldn't do it, because not only don't I get to say what I want to say, I'm getting so angry that I can't function the way I want to."

• "John, it's clear that you're upset by what Ralph is saying. But you are accusing him of not being honest, and I don't think you can be sure whether Ralph is being honest or not in what he is saying. You have no way of knowing."

• "I think we ought to take a look at what has been happening here. We seemed a minute ago to be close to a decision, but Jeanine didn't go along. When she expressed her objection, many of us began to put her on the spot by firing questions at her. Some of those questions sound pretty hostile. I think we ought to back off and consider what we want most: to put Jeanine down, or to arrive at the best possible decision."

The above are the kinds of comments that are made during the procedure we know as processing. Sensitivity training usually concerns itself more with process than with content and method. In fact, tasks, goals, or projects that a T-group undertakes—and the ways they are undertaken—are more for the purpose of generating interactions that can be processed than for the achievement of the task itself. It is probably true that most people do not really know how what they say and do affects other people. Just as hearing one's recorded voice for the first time can be shocking, or at least surprising ("I didn't know I sounded like that"), so can hearing that you have a tendency to use words or your body in such a way that you offend or irritate others.

Here is an illustration of what might go on in a typical T-group engaged in sensitivity training:

**Trust exercise.** One member of the group feels withdrawn or distrustful of other members. The others may feel difficulty in relating to or accepting that person. All consent to an exercise in which he lies on the floor surrounded by the other people in the group. They touch him or stroke him as they wish, and they may lift th person off the floor and hold him in the air for a few moments while he develops the trust that they will not drop him. After the exercise, he and others are encouraged to talk about their feelings during the event.

**Group decision-making.** One device used frequently through the years is the so-called NASA exercise: Participants, imagining themselves involved in a crash landing on the moon some distance away from their base, are given a list of supplies available in the wreckage and asked to rank those supplies in the order of their helpfulness in surviving the trek to the base (rope, radio, food, water, flashlights, etc.) First, each individual makes a ranking privately, then the group tries to arrive at a consensus through discussion of each member's own judgments. Usually the group's ranking will come closer than any individual's to that supplied by the space agency. What goes on between people during the discussion is fertile for processing: Who took over leadership? Who tried to dominate? Who withdrew from participation?

**Competitive games.** Sometimes an exercise is designed to provide an opportunity for two groups to work together, either cooperatively or against each other. One such exercise involves the distribution of money to all participants. Each group selects a negotiator. The two negotiators meet in a series of transactions to determine how the money will be used. A variety of transactions is possible, but there is a basic choice: either everyone in both groups winds up with the same amount he or she had in the beginning, or else one group conspires to manipulate the transactions to gain all or most of the money, thus depriving the members of the other group. In short, either no one loses, or one group wins while the other one loses. Much processing—and strong feelings, too—follow this kind of exercise.

A T-group may pass several days, or even two weeks, creating interactions, with the members exchanging feedback on the impact of the various behaviors and comments. The facilitator may choose to play a role as a member of the group, or may elect to be primarily an observer-processer. In the early stages of a group, the facilitator usually is needed to show group members how to give feedback and how to "level."

## Drawbacks

There's no question that the development of the T-group has been a significant one in research and application of the behavioral sciences. Since 1947 the sophistication of the approach has grown. Some organizations have experimented with sensitivity training internally. In the beginning, most such training was conducted in what are called "stranger" labs—where people may be literally strangers to one another, and certainly do not associate with one another on a regular basis. Internally, organizations have held "cousin" or "family" labs. The former are groups that work within the organization, but generally not with each other. They share a culture, but not much more. The family group consists of those who work together in the same department or division or in divisions that must work closely and regularly with one another.

But the unstructured T-group that characterizes sensitivity training has been heavily criticized in recent years. Among the most frequent charges leveled are these:

• The professional competence of the facilitator is often less than what is needed not only for the growth of the people in the T-group but also to handle occasional serious psychological problems that emerge in some participants.

• Sensitivity training outside of the organization creates an artificial atmosphere in which people feel supported, loved, trusted, to a degree not found in the real world. Hence, when T-group participants go back to that world, they have reentry problems, and often many of the positive feelings they had about the experience are dissipated.

• There is too much emphasis on *feelings* in family sensitivity training to the exclusion of other aspects of working together on the job. People sometimes report that their co-workers bare too much of themselves, resulting in the "I now know more about you than I care to know" feeling.

• Climates in organizations favor disguising of feelings, and suppression, not openness. So the opening up in T-groups will be heavily discouraged back on the work scene, even rebuked.

• People in sensitivity training spend too little time addressing themselves to solutions or decisions affecting organizational realities. It may be useful for personal growth and awareness, but the unstructured aspect of sensitivity training has little value for improving the effectiveness of the organization. It really does not *train.*

These are some of the criticisms leveled against sensitivity training. Each undoubtedly has some justification in some time, in some place, with people. But there is no question about the importance of the T-group in increasing the awareness and growth potential of many people. In the 1960s there was a nearly explosive proliferation of many kinds of groups for many kinds of purposes—the encounter group associated with Esalen on the West Coast; the marathon, in which people try to break down barriers in perception and communication through fatigue; the "nudies," in which people shed clothes and "other" barriers. All of these came under the label of the Human Potential Movement.

But in many organizations, there was the belief that while groups could be effective training situations, something more structured than sensitivity training was needed.

# The Instrumented Laboratory

One attempt to provide structure and to channel interactions is the instrumented lab. The term "instrumented" refers to the use in the lab of forms and feedback devices called instruments. Some forms are used as part of the tasks that are assigned or taken on by the group—for example, the NASA exercise previously described. Another task might be to try to arrive at a consensus on the relative importance of factors contributing to creativity. Other forms might deal with real problems on the job—defining the problems, ranking them, etc.

Some instruments are used to evaluate the group's activities during a specified task—did the group stay on target; was the atmosphere tense or supportive; to what extent were the evaluator's ideas listened to? Finally, there are instruments for giving feedback to other participants— to what extent they had appeared supportive, initiated ideas, blocked, dominated, etc.

Many organizations using instrumented labs offer both a public or stranger lab—where the tasks are simulations and originate in the group—and team-building sessions—family labs in which the problems or tasks dealt with are real and originate in the organization. Team-building proponents feel that in team-building lab sessions, which are usually held away from the organizational site, people's behavior resembles that in the work situation. In the lab, it is felt, problem or obstructive behavior can be recognized, confronted, and dealt with in the group through the processes of leveling and feedback. Consequently, when the same behavior occurs on the job, feedback can be given there more comfortably and accepted with less feeling of threat.

Often a stranger lab, or sometimes a cousin lab, constitutes a team-building program's phase one. Since the tasks are *simulated* exercises (or if the participants do not have direct working relationships), the atmosphere, it is believed, is more conducive to developing leveling and feedback skills. Once people have become more accustomed to being open and honestly communicative with others, they undergo phase two, in which the problems are real and the participants interact both in the lab and on the job.

Many professionals believe there are certain advantages to the instrumented lab: The use of forms and procedures leads to more predictable and measurable results. Too, the use of well-designed instruments helps to control and channel the leveling and feedback and avoids some of the excessive, ad hominem attacks that sometimes occur in sensitivity training. Another point concerning the use of instruments: They remove from the lab a resemblance to a therapy group, with which sensitivity training labs are not infrequently confused. The structured design of the instrumented lab leads participants to deal with organizational problems and confines interactions to here and now, i.e., the processing is concerned with behaviors observed in the lab itself, rather than, as in therapy, a residue of there-and-then activity (outside the lab at a former time).

However, in team-building labs there will be emphasis upon problems that have existed in the organization. The group will be asked to come up with solutions to those problems and the means to accomplish those solutions; the group also will assign responsibilities and establish schedules. The behavior that is processed is here and now, although there is the widespread belief that behavior, while working on real problems in the lab, will resemble that practiced by the group members on the job.

Nevertheless, the evolution of the group as an entity, as a problem-solving, decision-making, functioning, managerial body is effective today in our organizations because of Kurt Lewin's research and the happy accidental birth of sensitivity training.

The evolution of the research into group dynamics—which, you will remember, is the behavior of people in small groups—has led to several significant benefits. For one thing, it is becoming more important to consider than the motivation of behavior, or the attitudes behind it. Guessing at what motivates someone to take a certain action borders on the psychoanalytic; it is not always a useful management function. Another benefit of training in group skills is the increased realization that one is confined by one's perceptions; that is, Irene can describe Harry's behavior only in terms of Irene's perceptions of that behavior and its impact on her. Irene may express her *beliefs* as to the effect of Harry's actions on another, but she cannot claim, with certitude or authority, "You are making Linda angry." Only Linda can affirm or deny Irene's perceptions.

The acceptance and expression of feelings is another enhancement of the recognition of group behavior—really, how people behave. The stereotype of the successful executive dominated organizational life for many years: "Let's try to keep emotions out of this." People who expressed strong emotions on the work scene—anger, frustration, shame, grief, hurt—were long considered, if they were women, "typically female"; if men, unstable.

People have been taught, in sensitivity training and labs, to accept the feelings of others without having to agree with such feelings. "Yes, I can see that you're angry." Or, "I can understand why you are upset." The legitimization of feelings, whereby people can be free both to express their feelings (rather than suppress them) and accept others' emotions without passing judgment on them, has to be one of the most important consequences of the evolution of the group as a training situation.

Another byproduct of group dynamics is the growing emphasis on experiential learning, which is basically learning by doing and then getting feedback on how well the

doing was done. Much of the professional and management training and development in organizations has been
traditional, modeled after education practices of decades—classrooms, books, simulated exercises, instruction
removed from the actual work environment. There has also
been continuing criticism of this form of education—hard-
to-measure results; the organization doesn't foster or reinforce practice of what is learned in the classroom; there's
often no incentive on the part of the student to learn, since
what is learned has too much of the academic or theoretical, too little of the useful.

It is safe to say that the learning potential of problem-solving, decision-making groups working on real organizational
issues has only barely been touched.

## Group Growth, Dynamics, and Skills

While it is true that each group is in some way different from
other groups, nonetheless it has been observed that some
meaningful generalizations can be made about groups and
how people tend to behave and interact in them. Furthermore, there are loosely defined stages in the growth of a
group toward effectiveness. These generalizations can be
important and useful to anyone who must work in and with
small groups. Ironically, in spite of the wealth of research in
group dynamics, even though the use of task forces, committees, and work teams seems to be on the increase in all
kinds of organizations, training in group skills—techniques
for working constructively with others to achieve a common
objective—is surprisingly haphazard. The *content* is the
one aspect considered most important, since courses and
seminars devote much time to how to define a problem.
There is admittedly some concern devoted to the techniques, the *method* of decision-making. But the third aspect of group problem-solving and decision-making, *proc-*

*ess,* is often left to chance by being largely neglected in training. Process, you will recall, has to do with the behavioral interactions between members of the group.

There are, in the evolution of most groups toward effectiveness in the accomplishment of whatever their tasks may be, several stages that can be fairly well identified and defined. Being able to recognize these stages in the progress of a group can contribute to the constructive leadership and participation that lead to further development. Not recognizing the steps in group growth can lead to frustration, dissension, obstructive behavior by various members, and sometimes even to abandonment of the group and its task. For example:

1. The initial phase in the operation of a new group is often characterized by confusion—roles to be played by the members, the task to be performed, the type of leadership and where it is to come from. People may have been given definite assignments to be members of the group, but they do not yet perceive themselves as part of it. The group at this point is largely a collection of individuals. It is a *searching* phase. "What are we really here for?" "What part shall I play?" "Why was I appointed?" "Why were these others designated?" "Why is the leader our leader? What are his or her qualifications?" "Who is going to tell us what we are supposed to do?"

In the searching stage, much of what goes on between people is ostensibly centered on the task to be performed by the group. The interactions may carry some *noise*—that is, they may reflect biases and preconceptions and antagonisms formed before the group came together. But there is some content; that is, what is said will be concerned with what the group is to consider its work.

2. Stage two usually is reached after there has been an acceptable definition of the problem or the objective of the group. Sometimes the problem will be defined essentially as it was by the authority that established the group. Or it

will be explained by the formally appointed leader and consist of that person's understanding of what it is all about. Too, a definition may be constructed piecemeal—this person's interpretation supplemented by that person's.

Phase two sees the emergence of identifiable interactions. Often conflicts emerge between those members who want to get the job done quickly and those who feel that more time and deliberation are advised. Some members of the group can be expected to apply solutions they have brought with them, while others will worry as to whether the issue has actually been defined correctly and realistically. There will be members who want a strong, somewhat autocratic leadership, and others who would prefer that a more democratic, open atmosphere be maintained.

In this stage, one often sees a clash of personal agendas. Such agendas are those that members have brought into the conference room. They may be quite simple: One member wants to act in such a way as to attract the attention and admiration of a power figure in the group. Another person, wanting to achieve a position of leadership, wants to be seen as the informal, perhaps actual, leader. Personal agendas can be very complex: One member sees the group forum and membership as an opportunity to obtain hearing and consideration of a favored project of hers that is broader and more far-reaching than the assigned task of the group. This member may spend much of her time—and that of the group—trying to persuade others to redefine the task so as to get her project on the formal agenda.

Some of the conflicts and personal agendas may be dealt with openly—that is, they will be recognized and confronted. For example, when a personal agenda is suspected and defined by another person, the member who has been operating by it may be persuaded to deemphasize it. Or the member may decide to bury it until later and reintroduce it. A conflict may be honestly resolved. On the other hand, it may just be suppressed for a time.

However, it is characteristic of many groups at this stage that personal agendas and conflicts are often not resolved or even recognized. If they are not, chances are good that they will be manifested later. What often happens is that leadership—task-oriented leadership, usually—will emerge to get the group moving again toward its objective. *Processing* will be discouraged, except in a group in which the members are skilled in that activity. Interestingly, the leadership that moves the group back onto the track without attempting to resolve some of the process problems may well be resented later, once the members have come to appreciate how important it is to deal with the interactions between people as well as the content.

3. The group now begins to approach *coalescence*. Members may sense that they are no longer a collection of personalities in a room but that their behavior is influenced by their membership in this particular group and by interactions with other members. There is a growing commitment to the objectives of the group. There is also some attention given to process, because there is a desire to help people be more effective. There is a realization that unresolved conflicts, and personal issues not confronted by members, can obstruct progress toward those objectives.

Up to the point of coalescence, the group may have been fragmented. Either each member retained individuality, or power subgroups were obstacles to group wholeness. Much of this fragmentation begins to fade as the group takes on an identity and a personality of its own. People now hope there may be a sufficient unity to get the job done, to accomplish the objective.

4. Groups that continue for a period of time, that are engaged in complex tasks, get considerably beyond the coalescence phase. They become concerned with how to increase their effectiveness, on this job as well as on others. Getting the job done is one thing; another is learning how to be more skilled at getting the job done. Groups at this stage

often become self-evaluative. Evaluation methods to enhance this process is a subject we shall return to.


# Group task and building functions

There are generally two different kinds of functions exer-
cised by members in each of the stages of a group: *task*
roles, which involve furthering the group's success in
reaching the stated objective, and *building-maintenance*
roles, which have to do with increasing and maintaining the
group's effectiveness in its work as a group.

Some examples of task roles:

**Confronting issues.** Example: two departments that
work together are having problems in cooperation. They
may try, as many groups do, to avoid the real problems that
they create between themselves. One way of doing this is
to blame everything on a third department instead of blam-
ing each other. The way to confront is to ask such questions
as, "What thing are *we* doing to create problems that we
should stop doing?" Or, "What areas of cooperation are we
not covering now that we could?"

**Initiating ideas.** People who come up with new ideas,
suggestions, and proposals without censoring themselves
or worrying about how others will receive them are invalu-
able to the group.

**Pointing out the need for clarification and data-seek-
ing.** This role demands that a suggestion or a proposal be
expanded and supported by data, that all questions arising
in connection with it be answered or at least discussed, and
that everyone understand what is involved.

**Developing alternatives.** One legitimate complaint that
has been leveled against many groups is that they tend too
quickly to settle on one solution before all of the options
have been presented and explored. Thus, members who

assume the role of insisting that sufficient time and opportunity be given for exploration and development of alternatives play an important part in the group's success in accomplishing its task effectively.

**Integrating ideas.** Many seemingly divergent ideas and proposals, if carried far enough, if explained sufficiently, grow closer together rather than farther apart. This role has to do with finding similarities rather than differences.

**Evaluating.** Not only must options be introduced, they have to be evaluated as to their appropriateness to the group's mission. Ideas very often sound better than they are, or else, introduced by an authority or an otherwise especially respected figure, they are not given proper thought. The role of evaluator is therefore essential to group task accomplishment. Closely related to the evaluative role is that of *feasibility tester.* This person asks that the group consider just how feasible is a given proposal, considering the conditions and circumstances of the reality in which the proposal is to be applied.

**Dominating.** This is often seen as a negative, unhelpful role. But there are times when the group flounders, or when the group leader carries the group toward the wrong goal or toward a personal objective. In such an instance the member who can assume a temporary leadership by dominating the deliberation can play a positive role. It is when the domination becomes permanently established or is for the achievement of a personal agenda that the function becomes an obstacle to getting the proper job done.

**Keeping the group on target.** This is a delicate role. There are people who seem intolerant of an open-ended, unstructured discussion. However, such a discussion might be the only way that options can be recognized, in which case a target-oriented member can be counted on to try to coax the group back to a well-defined channel. On the other hand, groups can be diverted to unprofitable sidings—for example, by a conflict that strays off course.

Or perhaps the group discusses items that some members feel have little relevance. Any time a member suggests to the group his or her feeling that the discussion has departed from the course that leads to the objective, that person is fulfilling this group-task role.

The above are some task roles that can be performed by any member of the group, not only by the appointed or formal leader. In addition to group-task roles, there are certain functions that contribute to the effective functioning of the group as a group.

Some examples of group building and maintenance roles are:

**Encouraging.** People—especially those new to the group experience—need to be encouraged to speak up without fear of censoring or censure. For that matter, almost anyone needs some encouragement in a risk-taking situation, which is what most groups of people are in. When a member is hesitant, or seems withdrawn, or takes time to get thoughts out, another can step in and let the member in difficulty know that his or her contribution is welcome. Similarly, when people are performing in ways that benefit the group, those activities should be favorably commented upon.

**Harmonizing.** When things become very tense and tempers and feelings are high, the harmonizer steps in, not to shut off discussion, but to find the salient points of agreement or near-agreement. Sometimes the harmonizer doesn't dwell upon the content but finds something light or humorous to say that relieves the tension. The harmonizer has to be careful that the humor doesn't put people down or denigrate a point of view.

**Mediating.** In this role of group building and maintenance the member sets out to find ways to resolve—or at least to soften—an argument or seemingly disparate views of two or more other members. Often people within a group will debate for a long, wasteful period without realizing they are not substantially far from occupying the same position.

Or they will get hung up on non-essential points that conceal the fact that on the essentials they are close to agreement. Too, they may be discussing points that are off-course. The mediator steps in to ease the situation by demonstrating that the debate isn't really necessary or helpful; this is done without shutting if off or ridiculing the disputants.

**Expediting.** This function used to be described as gatekeeping, that is, keeping the gate from being closed to anyone. No one person or group should be permitted to dominate to the point that some people are shut out of the debate or discussion. If someone has been shut out, a member should assume the responsibility for interceding, for making sure everyone has access to the deliberations. Some group-behavior specialists, however, see gate-keeping as maintaining control negatively, keeping out participants who—or whose views—are disliked. So this role of safeguarding the participation of all is better referred to as expediting.

**Supporting.** In this role one member supports another, as to either the position advanced or the value of the contribution. In group dynamics, the opposite of supporting is competing. People in a supportive atmosphere feel that their contributions are valued and that therefore *they* will be valued by others. In a competitive environment members may feel that others regard them as a threat and fear their contributions.

**Listening.** Sometimes it is important for a member to make sure that the group hears another member. People closely involved in a discussion sometimes have too much invested in their own feelings and opinions to hear clearly what others are saying. Often they presume that others are rebutting them, when in fact that may not be true. "I'm not sure you heard what John said. What I heard him say is . . ." is the kind of function that makes sure people get heard, that valuable time is not spent debating points that were not really made.

**Supplying methodology.** The member who says, "Let's go around the table and ask everyone to comment on this issue with a maximum limit of five minutes per person," or "I suggest we decide this matter by consensus rather than majority vote," is providing methodology. Groups may get so wrapped up in the intricacies of the contest or in processing that they lose sight of how they can get on dealing practically with the issues.

**Processing-Observing.** There are many ways that this role can be fulfilled. Anyone who asks, "What's really happening here," or comments, "I think we ought to ask what is going on. What I see happening is John coming down very hard on Al and no one doing anything to help Al get on his feet," is fulfilling that role. Many people seem to assume that the most valuable processing takes place when things are going wrong or when people are being negative in their dealings with one another. Just as important, and in some ways more so, is the processing that takes place when things are going especially well, when people are interacting in a very constructive, furthering, nurturing manner. When such interactions and behaviors are pointed out, the whole group can improve its effectiveness by observing and repeating the kinds of actions that have just been pointed out as helpful.

## Not-so-Helpful Behaviors

There is another, all-too-frequent kind of occurrence that can spell trouble for a group: the hidden agenda. It is very like the personal agenda. In fact, some hidden agendas are personal agendas. What difference there is between the two can be explained this way: The personal agenda may not be covert. It may be quite obvious; its owner makes no effort to hide it. For example, a committee is planning an off-site meeting place for the field sales force. One member suggests a lodge in New Hampshire. "It's a good meeting place, and it will enable me to take some time off after the meeting and do some skiing." That qualifies as a personal agenda—open, but subjective.

A hidden agenda, on the other hand, may be difficult to discover. For example, Rita and Helen are invited to be members of the same task force. Rita feels that Helen is a potential competitor for a promotion that Rita knows will open up soon. Rita wishes to undermine Helen's chances to compete successfully, and is a persistent critic of Helen's contributions to the task-force deliberations. Presumably Helen's ideas and suggestions are subject to being evaluated and critiqued just like anyone else's. Therefore it is difficult to realize—unless it is known that Rita fears Helen's competition—that Rita has a hidden agenda, and that her criticisms are meant not to help the group but to hurt Helen.

Hidden agendas can be difficult to deal with. Sometimes they shouldn't be dealt with at all, just allowed to work themselves out. In other cases, when they are suspected, attention should be called to the fact and the issue squarely faced by the members of the group. Other obstructive activities that group members resort to are:

**Shutting off.** This can be done by devastation: "That's the most asinine idea I've ever heard." It can also be accomplished by interrupting, so that the feelings or ideas never get expressed.

**Judging behavior.** Saying such things to another as "You're defensive" or "You're projecting" only exacerbates the problem the person had expressing himself or herself. There is no sure way we can tell what motivates another's behavior.

**Analyzing behavior.** "Why are you so threatened?" may win an answer, a personal denial that will serve to sidetrack the discussion. Playing psychoanalyst may be exciting—but it usually doesn't advance the cause of the group.

**Blocking.** This term covers any device—humor, ridicule, raised voice, personal argument—that serves to deflate or bury what a person is saying. The primary objective in blocking is to keep the other from being effective, keep him from being heard or taken seriously.


## Group Evaluation

After a group has been operating for a time, and when its members are very conscious of the need to measure and give feedback on the way they do their work in the group, it is desirable to have a method of evaluating the effectiveness of the group. Not only does evaluation guide the group to greater effectiveness, but it also helps members sharpen their skills for the future.

Some of the questions that group members should answer are:

- How successful is the group in defining the problem?
- Did the group make efforts to develop as many options as possible?
- How effective is the group in utilizing the available resources to insure the widest possible consideration of the options?
- To what extent are the members' views considered by the group?
- How clear are the group's goals?
- To what extent have members' expectancies of the group's goals and progress been realized?
- How relevant are the group's discussions to the stated objectives?

- How successful are the group's efforts to resolve conflicts among the members?
- What is the atmosphere of the group's deliberations? Is it, e.g., tense, supportive, open, relaxed, competitive?

These are the kinds of questions that periodically can be asked, recorded, even discussed. Out of the records and/or discussions can come the material that will guide the group toward greater effectiveness.

The foregoing are functions that can—and should—be performed by any member of the group. But there is another kind of role: group leadership.

## Group Leadership

Its nature depends largely upon the purpose of the group. It is a great deal more than observing parliamentary procedure. If the group is a problem-solving, decision-making one, then there are, in addition to the roles that other participants also perform, these functions:

**State the problem.** It requires considerable skill to put the problem or the issue under discussion in such a way as not to impose unnecessary constraints or guide the deliberations in a direction favored by the leader. However, what is essential is that all of the constraints and limitations in the mandate from management be expressed: "We have no more than $120,000 to work with."

**Restate the problem.** After the group has applied brain power, the problem may assume different proportions, and it is necessary to recognize the change: "We started out trying to make the Main Street operation profitable, but now we find that what is needed first is a set of criteria to help us clearly establish the profitability of all of our branch operations."

**Summarize.** This is a leadership function that is useful

not only to establish or reestablish perspective but also to provide some sign of progress that can encourage further deliberation.

**Test commitment.** One role that a leader can do perhaps better than anyone else is to find out just how committed people are to the ideas, solutions, and decisions being discussed.

**Confirm the consensus.** If everyone's understanding, agreement, and support are desired, the leader must make sure that all pre-decision conflicts have been resolved. He or she may have to slow up progress or go over previously covered material to accomplish this. Otherwise the members may experience cognitive dissonance.

**Ensure use of all resources.** The group cannot be sure of making the best decision unless all of the talents and abilities available to the group—both inside and outside— are utilized. The leader should catalogue these resources and make sure they have been called upon.

**Share leadership.** One way the leader can ensure the proper utilization of the resources within the group is to make every effort to share the power. There may be an aspect of a problem calling for a certain skill or knowledge that one member has a greater amount of. This specialist should be encouraged to play a major role in the discussion or other work relating to that aspect. More generally, all of the members of the group should be encouraged to play a constructive role.

Leadership in such group situations as those described is just one aspect of the overall reexamination of the nature of management. That leadership skills are changing cannot be denied. After all, the work force is radically different from what it was even twenty years ago. People's perceptions of themselves as members of organizations have been altered substantially. New forms of structuring organizations, as we shall see, are being experimented with. Clearly, there is a demand for new kinds of thinking about what it takes to be a good leader.

# The New Leadership

It was Kurt Lewin who developed the triple definition of management styles: *autocratic,* keeping power to oneself, issuing commands, refusing to share leadership; *democratic,* sharing power, inviting subordinates to have a say in the issues that affect them; and *laissez faire,* the free-rein approach, letting employees have their head.

In the early days of research into leadership, great emphasis was placed on categorizing managerial style. Perhaps no approach to classifying style has ever been so widely received and—for a time—influential as the Managerial Grid.

## Blake, Mouton, and the Grid

The Managerial Grid (figure 11), brainchild of Robert R. Blake and Jane Srygley Mouton, was truly a phenomenon of the early 1960s. The interest in group dynamics was growing, along with suspicions that sensitivity training was not going to be the answer to organizational change. There had been for some time a preoccupation with leadership style—what kinds of direction and interactions with subordinates would result in the most productive performance. Then too, Douglas McGregor had made a tremendous impact with Theory Y.

The two polarities expressed by the Grid are reminiscent of McGregor: a manager's *concern for production* or *concern for people.* Concern for production has to do with efforts that directly result in whatever the organization is designed to manufacture and/or sell, be it a product or a service.

*Concern for people* is expressed in such terms as responsibility, accountability, trust, building constructive interactions between people, providing reward systems for effort, a congenial environment, enhancing the self-esteem of employees, etc.

The vertical axis indicates concern for people, while the horizontal axis measures concern for production. One purpose of the Grid is to help managers define that style which is dominant in them. What follows is a brief description of the five management nomenclatures devised by Blake and Mouton.

9,1 This orientation reflects a high concern for production and a very low concern for people. This is a task-oriented person—getting the job done is the most important thing. Of course, one must use people to get the work out, but the 9,1 boss would like to utilize employees much as machines. The 9,1 managers probably view themselves as firm, rational people. But emotions and feelings are out. There is neither time nor room for people to express themselves, their desires, and their needs, for that could get in the way of doing a good job on schedule.

The 9,1 boss plans and orders. Subordinates listen and

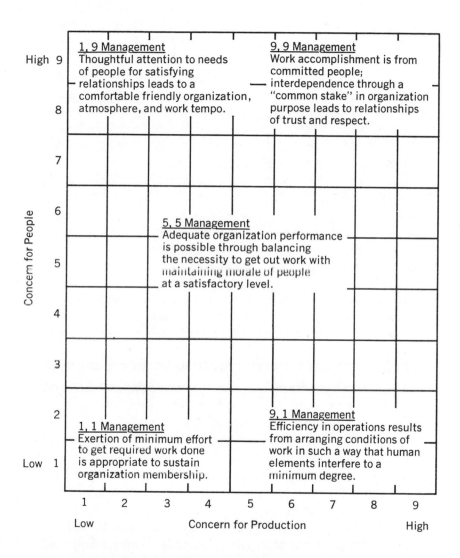

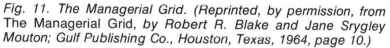

*Fig. 11. The Managerial Grid. (Reprinted, by permission, from* The Managerial Grid, *by Robert R. Blake and Jane Srygley Mouton; Gulf Publishing Co., Houston, Texas, 1964, page 10.)*

do what they're told to do. The manager knows best. (The 9,1 corner is where we would expect to find the stereotype entrepreneur.) People are expected to accept the manager's superior wisdom and competence. Even if they don't, they'd better believe that this boss has authority, which is not shared. The employees who do as they are told stay on the manager's good side; those who question, talk back, or try to deviate from the boss's plans or methods are insubordinate and should be punished. When mistakes are made, much effort is expended to assign blame.

Because of the overriding concern for production, feelings—including conflicts, anger, and hostility—are repressed. The 9,1 manager has one way of dealing with such disruptions: "If you don't like it here and can't get along, go somewhere else." Rules and standard operating procedures are imposed on everyone, with rare exceptions. People who work for this manager know what they must or must not do. No such restrictions tie the manager, who is free to manipulate and does not see himself as having to be open or honest with subordinates. The end justifies whatever works.

The primary flow of information is downward. A little goes up, usually what employees can't keep hidden or what they think the boss wants to hear. The horizontal flow is either non-existent or highly obstructed.

9,1 management is extremely autocratic. Strong, informal groups of employees tend to exist under this kind of manager; their purpose is to express anti-organizational feelings. There are, predictably, a rather low commitment and loyalty to the organization. The attitude prevalent among employees is: "Give the boss what you have to and no more." Behavior reflecting this attitude simply reinforces the Theory X assumptions about people that 9,1 managers usually have.

1,9 This orientation reflects a low concern for production and a high concern for people. This manager, not wishing to appear pushy or dictatorial, works hard not to offend employees. The 1,9 style comes close to what Kurt Lewin described as laissez faire. This boss is compassionate, understanding, at times paternal. Most employees of 1,9 managers probably feel it is impossible to work for anyone nicer. Conditions, the work environment, are high-priority items. The 1,9 boss requests, suggests, even apologizes for expectations. This manager dislikes conflict and unpleasantness just as much as the 9,1 boss. However, 1,9 managers don't seek to repress it. Their strategy is to avoid the seeds of it: "We're a big, happy family." When these bosses are crossed or disappointed, they may show more hurt and sorrow than anger. High value is placed on personal loyalty and morale. There is no need for unhappiness and dissension because there has to be a way that everyone can be made happy, and room for everyone to do his or her thing. There's much smoothing over.

Communications upward reflect happy conditions. Bad news would usually be censored out. There is a horizontal flow, much of it social in nature rather than work-related.

It's always possible that employees of a 1,9 manager may worry about the boss's relationship with other managers in the organization, his eagerness to accommodate, to be seen as a nice person. They may wonder whether the boss caves in quickly to avoid being seen as aggressive and as a troublemaker or boat-rocker. Blake and Mouton describe this boss as a "country club" manager.

1,1 These managers have little concern for production *or* people. 1,1 managers withdraw. Their basic concern is with protection and survival of self. They give very little of themselves, ask little of anyone else. This is a let's-get-by-as-best-we-can style. Blake and Mouton describe the 1,1 as a message carrier, passing to employees what comes down from above: "Look, don't blame me. This is what they want done." If it isn't done, 1,1 says to superiors, "I told them. But what can you expect from people like that?"

This manager's goals are personal—keep the job, collect the pay, get a pension. To accomplish those ends, they stay out of the way, don't make waves, get along and go along. "Don't take risks—that's what could get you into trouble." Such a boss is passive, uninvolved, out of it. He or she is not concerned with results as much as with avoiding criticism. Thus, 1,1 managers keep records not in order to plan production and performance, but to provide proof that they have done what they were supposed to do. They avoid conflicts by not taking a stand, ignoring unpleasantness or letting others work things out. In fact, the 1,1 lets others do most of everything.

9,9 This position on the Grid indicates a high concern for both people and production. This boss feels that production and people are strongly related, that people want to produce, to be effective, to get results from their efforts. The people in it fulfill Theory Y assumptions. Their needs are high up on Maslow's hierarchy.

The 9,9 manager creates working conditions in which people know what is required and what is going on; conditions where people contribute ideas, know those ideas are important, and therefore have a stake in the outcome. People are supportive of the operation and of each other. They participate in the decisions that affect them. They work hard so that the solutions they themselves helped formulate can work.

There is a recognition by the 9,9 boss that people fulfill many of their needs and goals on the job. And the 9,9 manager looks for ways to help them do just this. He coordinates, rather than controls. He or she recognizes that full and complete communicating helps spark motivation, competence, and commitment. Well-informed employees do better work, because they understand organizational goals.

The 9,9 managers look to remove obstacles to effective performance. They see themselves as resources for employees. They delegate, encourage innovation. When mistakes occur, the manager is less interested in pointing a finger of blame than in making sure that learning has resulted from the error, which therefore is less likely to occur again.

Goals are discussed with employees—and jointly set where possible. In the 9,9 orientation, therefore, it is important that goals be clear, realistic, "owned" by everyone. Conflict and problems are inevitable in a progressive organization of people. There are opportunities for doing things better than before. Trust is very important in this orientation; manipulation and deception have no place.

Communications are three-way—up, down, sideways. Their purpose is to help employees to be more effective. Such communications are open, authentic, candid: Issues and conflicts are confronted by the people involved. Creativity is high under a 9,9 boss. Interactions are encouraged; team action and supportive behavior are what the 9,9 boss seeks to build.

5,5  This manager's moderate concern for both people and production is a halfway act. It is probably more pragmatic than anything: a concern for people as producers. The 5,5 Grid position probably, in Likert's terms, overlaps Systems 3 and 4. The reasons for doing things are explained, and there may be some consultation and discussion.

The 5,5 manager acts in conformity with traditions, rules, and regulations. Organizations with a dominant 5,5 style, therefore, are bureaucratic. The performance standards may be mediocre: They do not encourage excellence nor are they tolerant of poor work. There are probably strong cultural norms: People know what kind of dress is frowned upon, what language is acceptable, what protocol is practiced.

Goals are discussed. Communicating organizational objectives undoubtedly is more important than considering individuals' goals. Conflict is not confronted. The prescription for conflict resolution is to back off and let people cool. Compromise is the desirable kind of solution.

Much effort goes into maintaining conditions as they are—and have been. Staying in line is encouraged. Carrot-and-stick is the leadership style.

Most people in organizations in recent years would recognize the prevalence of the 5,5 style.

## The Grid Seminar

Blake and Mouton also developed a design for what was called a seminar, although it is much closer to an instrumented laboratory. The objective of the seminar is to give people an opportunity, through self-assessment and feedback from others, to define their own styles and to work on problems using the attributes of a 9,9 orientation.

There is no question but that the Grid is a capital example of an approach that became widely adopted not necessarily because it offered a superior method of developing better managers, but because it was a confluence of several streams of work: the emergence of managers with Theory Y assumptions about people; group dynamics and sensitivity training; and human relations. And a *need:* to find some uncomplicated and practical way to express the store of theoretical knowledge that was building up and appealing to managers.

## Contingency Management

Another approach to developing leadership effectiveness is to try to develop the manager's ability to meet varying conditions. This is called situational leadership. A third in-teresting alternative has been proposed by Fred E. Fiedler of the University of Illinois and the University of Washington. His belief is that it is easier to adjust the situation than to change the leader. In Fiedler's perspective, three factors bear on a leader's effectiveness:

1. **Leader-member relations.** Leaders will have more power and influence with members of their groups if those leaders are liked, respected, and trusted by the members.
2. **Task structure.** A leader has more influence in tasks that are highly structured, explicit, or pro-grammed than in assignments that are vague, nebulous, and unstructured.
3. **Position power.** Leaders have more power and in-fluence if their position allows them to reward and punish, hire and fire.

The task can be adjusted to the leader's motivation, which will be either task-oriented or relationship-oriented. Fiedler's method for determining the orientation of a man-ager is to ask the manager to describe his or her *least-preferred co-worker*. A manager with a strong task orienta-tion perceives a least-preferred co-worker in generally un-favorable terms, while a relationship-oriented leader will employ more favorable terms of description.

Thus, in assigning managers, you would look for situations which would be more congenial to the managers' orienta-tions. A leader more concerned with task would probably perform better in highly structured or quantitative positions, such as accounting. Fiedler suggests that the task can be made to *seem* more structured. Presumably constraints, limits, and methods could be spelled out more in advance in some assignments than in others.

In a less-structured operation, such as sales or research, a relationship-oriented person might do a superior job. If the group to which the leader is to be assigned comprises highly motivated, self-actualizing employees, and the work to be done is varied, the manager should be one who leans toward the human-relations end of the spectrum. The employee mix can be changed, bringing in more people compatible with structuring—or the contrary.

The position power of the leader can be increased by, for example, providing the leader's operation with more autonomy or increased power to hire and fire over a time period.

Much of the contingency theory of Fiedler's is still to be refined and substantiated. But it is beyond question that Fiedler's theory opens to us another leadership option. We have to look beyond fitting the leader to the situation. Not only is the question, therefore, one of finding and training the leader most suitable, but also one of considering how the situation, the work group, the task, and the authority can be modified to suit the leader.

## Existential Management

Traditionally, in the eyes of psychologists Charles L. Hughes and Vincent S. Flowers, management imposed its value system upon employees. A manager set the goals, determined the procedures for achieving those goals, and established the working conditions under which the achievement would take place. But as Hughes and Flowers point out, employees have a wide range of values. For example, some of the value systems represented in the work environment are:

- **Tribalistic.** People holding these values prefer strong leadership—a chieftain. They like routine, repetitive tasks. They tend to seek approval from the boss.

- **Egocentric.** This is the rugged individualist. This person needs a strong boss, tight control, close supervision.
- **Conformist.** Oriented toward duty and loyalty, these people have a high regard for the work ethic.
- **Manipulative.** This is the wheeler and dealer. The manipulator looks for opportunities, higher prestige, money and other material rewards. This person needs a fair amount of room in which to operate.
- **Sociocentric.** People are the most important thing to this employee, who places a high value on interpersonal relationships, friendly supervision, harmony in the work group. Individual achievement is not a motivator.
- **Existential.** Concerned with themselves as individuals, these people look for enriched jobs and meaningful tasks. They thrive on challenge and want opportunities to participate in goal-setting.

Obviously, with so many value systems present, a *mirror manager* (Hughes's and Flowers's term for the manager who sees his or her own values mirrored everywhere) is not going to be generally effective in communicating, managing, and providing the appropriate leadership that encourages effective performance.

It is the conviction of these two psychologists that people should be placed in jobs and environments that match their values. But even when such a matching program can be developed, it is necessary for managers to recognize that their own values may not correspond to those of some of their subordinates. Thus we have the *existential manager.* This manager sets the goals for the organization. He—or she—then shares with employees information about methods, constraints, limitations on available resources, etc. Finally, the manager provides opportunities for employes to become involved, to participate in the design of the systems and procedures they will use to achieve the goals that management has established. That way, people with disparate value systems can have a say in setting systems, procedures, working conditions that are more compatible with those values than if a manager had unilaterally established them.

Thus, as management thinking evolves, we are getting further away from the traditional concepts of style to the need for managers to make appropriate responses to employees who think and behave according to different sets of values. However, managers tend to have a certain style in dealing with people, a style that reflects their own values, how they feel about themselves, their work, their co-workers. There is no such thing as a "universal" manager who can relate in the same way with everyone. So it is extremely important for managers to recognize the behavior that is predominant in the employees. Only by such recognition can they know how to change or vary behavior situationally.

And, as Fiedler points out, it is possible to structure the environment to match the leadership style of a particular manager.

The options for achieving more effective management are increasing through the research of the behavioral scientists—but so are the complications.

# The Effective Organization

Chris Argyris, the noted consultant, prolific author, and Harvard professor, seemingly has spent much of his professional career searching for the effective organization—which, in his eyes, is one that increases output while maintaining or decreasing input—or maintains output while decreasing inputs. The "inputs" are the energies people put into whatever it is that the organization does. Unfortunately, Argyris feels that much of this energy may go to accomplish things that are not the organization's objectives. At lower levels, for example, employees slow down their production, hold a lid on the rate, cheat on production records. There is goldbricking and widespread noninvolvement.

The situation that exists in many organizations in which people work frustrates what in Argyris's mind is the natural development of the personality. Argyris has defined seven growth stages, starting with infancy and immaturity—with their dependence upon others, the ability to behave in only a few ways, having shallow, short-term interests, showing a lack of awareness of self—and progressing to these more mature characteristics:

- Independence of others;
- Variety of behaviors;
- Deeper, long-term interests and investments of energy;
- Looking for rewards in doing things for their own sake;
- Aspiring to occupy an equal or subordinate position relative to peers;
- Seeking control over areas in which they can decide.

The mature individual, in Argyris's theory, seeks more responsibility, more decision-making powers. This search culminates either in activities that contribute to the organization of which the person is a member, or in efforts that may even work against the organization's welfare. For example, at the supervisory level there are efforts to hide what goes on—or doesn't go on!—at the lower levels. There is interdepartmental conflict and rivalry, poor decision-making, management by crisis.

At the upper levels, activity is characterized by politicking and a high noise ratio—that is, communication that doesn't communicate anything significant of itself.

All of these so-called *unintended activities* (unintended by the organization, at least) consume energy. And activities that are designed to hide these unintended activities take further energy. You do these unintended activities—that's work of a sort. You hide the fact that you do them—that's also energy-consuming. The organizational objectives aren't getting the benefits of it. Not only that, but when people at every level see others instituting protective devices to conceal the ineffectiveness, they feel frustrated, distrustful, reinforced in their lack of involvement. The result will be a lack of motivation to at least work together—all parts of the organization—toward the achievement of the organizational goals.

For Argyris, moving from the less-effective organization toward that which is more effective involves leaving behind employee activities that fight one another, compete, are in conflict, are directed to achieving objectives that don't have much to do with where the total group should want to be. Argyris envisions an organized effort that is run for the welfare of all of the parts, not just some of them. He sees people as not coerced in their efforts, but collaborative, supporting each other in their contributions to the whole.

People *can* be coerced by others. They can also be *made* to cooperate. But to collaborate—that's an individual, personal decision. To collaborate in the achievement of organizational goals is a commitment that the employee makes.

How can employees be persuaded, induced, encouraged, to commit themselves to work for organizational effectiveness? One answer is that people are concerned about the outcome of their efforts—and want to have a say in how those efforts are expended. The most effective organization, therefore, in the eyes of social scientist Rensis Likert, is one in which employees have a voice in their work and in the organizational decisions that affect that work.

## Likert and System Four

Rensis Likert, former director of the Institute for Social Research at the University of Michigan, has been called "the father of participative management." Participative management is generally defined as a system in which people who will be affected by a decision are invited to share in the decision-making process. They are given a real voice, a chance to contribute ideas, to evaluate those of others, to join in the shaping of the outcome of the deliberations. Likert feels not only that better decisions come out of participation, but also that people are more highly committed to carrying them out. Involvement in a decision or an action that affects them gives employees a sense that they have some power over their destiny, that they can develop ways to realize their personal goals in working for organizational objectives—goals held by Argyris's "mature personality."

The most productive organization, in Likert's view, is what he calls participative group, or System Four. In this kind of organization decisions are better because the people who know the most about the issues join together in deciding. This is in contrast to the organization in which, say, marketing decisions are made or shared not by marketers but solely by executives at the top trained in law and/or finance.

Communications throughout are more effective in transmitting what the organization needs to know in order to function because the flow of information is up, down, and across. Not only are the lines and the transmission more complete than in the hierarchy in which the lines are mainly vertical, but also the information is more accurate. Management trusts those down the line and does not feel that letting go of data is tantamount to surrendering power and status. People on lower levels know how important it is to management to be apprised of what is going on, and they feel less hesitant to let management know all of the facts, not just the better-sounding ones. Motivation is stronger because the rewards for which people strive are based on the quantity and quality of their participation.

Likert's effective organization reflects a leadership style that he terms System 4. (The three other systems, or styles, that Likert views as frequent in organizations are exploitative-authoritarian, benevolent-authoritarian, consultative.)

There are three basic concepts of System 4:

1. The use by the manager of the principle of supportive relationships;

2. The manager's use of group decision-making and group methods of supervision;
3. High performance goals for the organization.

The first and third need some explaining. What is supportive is basically ego-building. The employee would experience in his interactions with others the kind of exchange that, in the light of the employee's background, values, and expectations, increase and maintain his sense of personal worth. Bosses and peers seek the employee's expertise, listen to him or her, and value the contribution. This kind of transaction is different from what many people experience and are accustomed to: "Learn your place and stick to it. If you don't do your job, we will find someone who will. You are paid to produce and not cause problems. You are not paid to think."

The System 4 organization sets objectives that, to the extent possible, reflect the needs and desires of the members, shareholders, customers, suppliers, and others who deal with it. Everybody benefits. Everyone is provided for, valued, and looked out for.

Likert maintains that, as with the case of Douglas McGregor's Theory Y, managers view System 4 as the one in which they believe they can operate more effectively. To confirm this, he conducted research using material formulated into what is known as the "Likert instrument"—forty-three operating characteristics arranged in an evaluation form. In the research, managers were asked to rate organizational variables in terms of how effective they seem in motivating worker productivity. Their choices of "most productive," "least productive," etc. are marked on a line representing a scale of effectiveness.

One variable might list "fear" at the extreme left of the line dealing with, for example, the way to run an organization; "compensation and participation" conceivably could be at the opposite end of that scale. According to Likert, most managers marked the left-hand characteristics as "least

productive," the right-side listings as "most productive"—
and these correspond, respectively, to System 1 and System 4 characteristics.

General descriptions of Systems 1 through 4 are as follows:

**System 1**—*Exploitative authoritative.* Management does not trust subordinates. Subordinates are not free to discuss matters with supervisors, nor are their opinions sought in solving problems. Motivation comes from fears, threats, occasional rewards. Communication comes down from higher management. The information that goes up from lower levels tends to be inaccurate. Goals are ordered from on high, where all of the decisions are made. The informal groups in the organization tend to exist in opposition to the wishes of higher management.

**System 2**—*Benevolent authoritative.* Management and employees exist in a master-servant relationship. There is some involvement of employees; more rewards than in System 1; slightly better communications up. This is a paternalistic organization, not unfriendly, as System 1 is, but without much latitude given to employees to do their thing.

**System 3**—*Consultative.* Management keeps control of things, but there is consultation with employees before solutions to problems and decisions are made by management. Communication upward is better, but it is still cautious. Unpleasant or unfavorable information is not freely offered. Employees have the feeling they will perform some roles in preliminary stages of decision making and policy setting but that their contributions may not be taken seriously all the time. Informal groups may go along with the formal organization or exist in opposition to management policies.

**System 4**—Management trusts employees, regards them as working willingly toward the achievement of organizational objectives. People are motivated by rewards.

At all levels they are involved in discussing and deciding those issues that are important to them. Communication is quite accurate and goes up, down, and across. Goals are not ordered from on high but are set with the participation of the people who will have to work to achieve them. Informal organizations are benign—they support the formal organization.

## The Linking Pins

The means by which members of a System 4 organization achieve not only such excellent communications, but also participation in those decisions that affect them, is the "linking-pin" structure. Each work group—defined as a superior and all subordinates who report to him—is linked with all levels of the hierarchy and with every other work group. Figure 12 is the way it would be pictorially represented.

Peer-group loyalty and collaboration are strong in a System 4 environment. Competition and distrust between peers, Likert feels, result in hoarding information, withholding assistance, etc. Instead, people should be encouraged to believe that the setting and fulfillment of organizational goals by all members of the organization aid in the satisfaction of individual goals. Thus it is to the benefit of each person that he or she share information, knowledge, expertise, and experience with everyone else who could benefit by that sharing.

Through the linking-pin type of structure, important issues can be recognized and dealt with instead of buried or ignored. People who have responsibility for some project or phase of work can maintain contact, even exercise coordination with others over whom they have no authority but who are also involved.

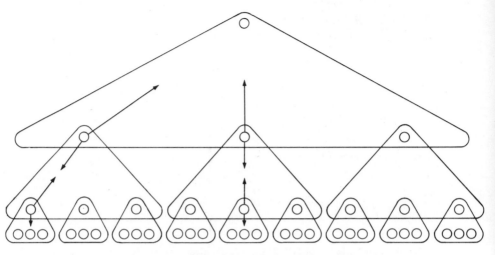

**(The arrows indicate the linking-pin function)**

*Fig. 12. The linking-pin structure. (Reprinted, by permission, from* New Patterns of Management, *by Rensis Likert; McGraw-Hill Book Company, New York, 1961, page 134.)*

The linking-pin concept demands flexibility—and familiarity with the group process. There are those who believe that the future will demand organizations even more flexible, even more expert in dealing with groups. Thus we have the concept of the Matrix.

## The Matrix Organization

In 1968, Warren Bennis, now president of the University of Cincinnati, wrote—together with sociologist Philip E. Slatter—a book called *The Temporary Society,* in which they speculated on the nature and problems of the organization of the future. Bennis took the view then that the classical, functional, hierarchical, pyramidal structure that most of us are familiar with would give way to a more democratic, decentralized system with small, temporary, problem-solving groups forming the authoritative heart of the organization. Of course, managers of the future might find it hard to give up their boxes on the organizational chart, their names and titles on the door, the fixed place and clear status on the vertical lines extending from top to bottom. Perhaps even more difficult would be the necessity of speedily making temporary affiliations with groups, and then leaving them to work with other groups.

Bennis has since modified his views and predictions: The trend toward democratization and "the temporary society" is not pronounced. Yet, many executives are concerned about a number of factors that militate against the perpetuation of the old-style authoritarian pyramid. Among them are:

• The need to bring technical or professional expertise closer to the decision-making powers. Often the people who know about the issue to be decided or the problem to be solved are not in on the decisional process. The people with decision-making authority are usually at some distance from the areas most affected by their actions.

• In today's fast-changing environment, information is money. In classical structures the flow of vital information is slow, restricted, and selective. What goes up to the decision-makers is censored; it comes out as what people below want known or believe higher management wants to hear. There is little provision for a steady and continuing horizontal exchange.

• Planning human resources has become an important, sophisticated field. Many specialists are coming to realize that both management and nonmanagement career-development paths should be lateral—sideways—as well as vertical, that the tightly compartmented structure does not provide the freedom and mobility desired.

Rensis Likert's System 4 is one approach to these concerns. Less elaborate answers are also available. Perhaps the one that was most demonstrated in the project management structure of the aerospace industry was the use of project management and teams: For each type of project there is a team, sometimes almost a company in miniature. For the duration of the project—or for whatever portion of time they were needed—a group of professionals was chosen to work on that project, usually on a full-time basis. The project team has a budget; it even, on occasion, negotiates with outsiders. Meanwhile, there is in the organization a permanent structure that provides continuity, finance, services, personnel, strategy, etc. In effect, there are two different organizations, one permanent, the other temporary. This kind of dual structure is referred to as a "matrix." (*Matrix,* in general, refers to that within which something forms or is given shape.)

The matrix takes whatever form it must to bring professional and technical expertise to bear on problems and projects. Thus in a matrix there will be some structures that are rigid and well defined, others that are less so. The more temporary aspects may be served by the project teams described above, or by an instrument more familiar to most, the task force.

The task force is generally defined as either part time or full time, temporary, semi-autonomous (it exists within the structure but with special or extraordinary operating authority from a high-level source), interdisciplinary, and interfunctional (people of different descriptions or professions and departments or divisions). Its purpose is to bring to bear optimal expertise. The task force differs from a committee in that it usually has decision-making power—and sometimes even the *responsibility* to implement its decisions.

A variation of the project team and the task force is the venture group, often used in the infant days of a new product, service, or enterprise. The team is responsible for the development, testing, and launching of the product or service. And if it takes off, the team may form the nucleus of the new, permanent management.

The work team is beginning to make its appearance in American manufacturing. The team usually comprises people who work together. They often determine assignments, scheduling, training, skills to be allocated, perhaps even rewards for performance and compensation for the next period. The work team in the U.S. is largely in an experimental stage. Evidence is limited, but early reports suggest that people who have substantial control over many aspects of their work—what they do,, when, and how find there is a significant effect on morale, motivation, and productivity.

The above are some of the variety of groups now being formed within classical hierarchical organizations to provide greater discretion for employees in shaping their work, and to bring to bear on a project or a problem the desirable amount of brainpower, a concentration that is difficult to accomplish in a more rigid organization.

## Organizations as Systems

Increasingly, social scientists are studying organizations in terms of systems theory, a relatively new discipline. A natural system can be defined as a complex organization of interdependent parts that together constitute a whole, each part contributing to the whole and receiving something from it, and the whole, in its turn, being interdependent with some larger environment. In systems theory there are three generally accepted models on which organizations are based:

**Mechanical.** This system of interrelated parts with a boundary usually tends to maintain an equilibrium. A building is a good example of a mechanical system: Its tensions and stresses keep the building in place. A mechanical system will tend to stay in its present state until compelled by some force to change. For example, a piece of machinery will remain motionless unless a switch is pulled, a push is given, a button is pressed.

**Organic.** Here one might think of a body, a biological system. A body has a relatively stable equilibrium—homeostasis—which is the resultant effect of continuous processes, such as temperature regulation in an animal. There is more capacity for alteration than in a mechanical system, but there are limits: An organic system cannot change its given structure *substantially.* Basically, the role of the organic system is maintenance of the system's status quo.

**Process.** In the process system the interrelationship with the environment is very complex and subject to changes. However, this system does not seek to maintain itself. It is adaptive, creating a new structure to better interact with forces that are pressuring for change. The system becomes more elaborate. At any time, therefore, the structure is temporary.

Systems theorists say that the mechanical represents a closed system, the process, an open one. Closed systems—and this description is admittedly oversimplified—work to minimize interactions with the environment. They tend not to welcome input from the outside. The energy goes to preserve the condition or the culture that exists on the inside. Of course, there is no completely closed system, but the label can be applied to an organization that venerates tradition, tries to reduce the influx of new ideas, is xenophobic—afraid of outsiders and the fresh thinking they represent.

In today's world, such a closed system is at a profound disadvantage. Markets change; prices, tastes, conditions vary. Technology races ahead. Energies generated from within to maintain relatively impermeable boundaries create entropy, a motion to destruction.

An open system, on the other hand, imports energy from outside itself. People depend upon stimulation from outside. Otherwise they do not grow. An open system not only interacts with the environment, it also seeks out those interactions that will be beneficial.

There is an exchange with the environment. Oxygen, for example, is brought into the lungs and expelled as carbon dioxide. A transformation occurs. The open system does not become unified with the environment, but the system takes it in as a contribution to its welfare. Raw material is received and is changed into something else. The needs of the open system are supplied by the environment; the latter is served by the system.

The open system will take in more from its environment than it expends, creating the means of its survival and growth. For example, the corporation takes in more money than it spends, thus creating profits and reserves. The open system, because of the variety of interactions with and responses to the environment, tends to become different in some way from other systems, closed or open. Such organizations move toward an elaboration of structure that encourages a multiplicity of functions and specializations. At given times it may be difficult, looking at the organization chart of such an entity, to determine everything that is going on—or precisely who is doing what.

Most organizations that we are familiar with are more closed than open. How the stimuli are responded to is usually determined by a narrow power center at the top. Therefore, depending upon how top management usually responds to information, people below will either suppress or else alter the information to make sure it gets a more favorable reception. What very often happens in the closed, bureaucratic system is that the response to information or challenge or stimulation is either nonexistent, inappropriate, or delayed.

In the change from a closed system to one that is open, the boundaries become more permeable. People at various levels receive authority and are trained to respond to the "environment" appropriate to their area of work, that is, the data relevant to their field of specialization, whether that be laws, markets, new technologies, competition, or natural events such as disasters and epidemics. To permit a faster reaction time or information flow, organizations tend to "flatten out." The pyramid loses its acutely angled lines and becomes flatter and broader based, with greater flexibility.

Thus, much of the thinking of organizational specialists appears to converge. This is *the temporary society* referred to by Warren Bennis in the book of that name. Decision-making power will be dispersed throughout the organization. People involved in specialized functions and projects, and who are affected by environmental change, will be able to respond effectively because they will have the power to do so. Expertise and specialization will be available where and when they are needed throughout the organization.

And there will be heavy, continuing use of project teams or task forces brought together to produce a product or a system, to solve problems or to make decisions.

Likert's System 4 incorporates many of the characteristics of the open system. The members of the groups are very much in contact with what is going on in the organization—and, to some degree, in the environment.

# Afterword

# Afterword: Organization Development

The behavioral science research, the theories, the techniques—what do all the preceding pages add up to? One answer might be Organization Development. Because Organization Development, or OD as its proponents refer to it, is concerned with *people and how they can be effective in organizations*. One definition: a planned, systematic, systemwide change to enable people to work more effectively for organizational goals. Whatever techniques, procedures, and processes are useful in helping members of an organization to improve upon their effectiveness in their work and in their interactions with others can be labeled OD technology. It is such a general technology that the term one often hears—OD specialist, denoting the person who is planning and/or implementing the change—is really a contradiction in terms because a number of specialties are involved. (The more correct title or term is "organization development practitioner.")

Many of the people who are going into OD work in organizations have backgrounds in the behavioral sciences. Universities now offer advanced-degree programs in OD, organizational behavior, and related areas of study and technology. High-level corporate titles such as "vice-president of human resources" have been created. Personnel and training functions are often found these days under the OD label. What used to be called manpower planning is now referred to as human resources planning. Clearly, our business, government, and not-for-profit institutions are definitely and permanently committed to finding better ways to utilize a resource—people—that until a few years ago was perhaps a low-priority concern.

OD itself has been taken seriously in the organizational world only in the past few years. During the 1960s, a mere handful of organizations and pioneers experimented with techniques such as team-building, sensitivity training, and conflict resolution. Some of that early experimentation seemed far out to many people. It was threatening because there was a lot of talk about relationships, the expression of feelings, leveling, changing behavior. To talk about OD in some work environments was to risk bringing some listeners to the point of hysteria.

Of course, not all of the hysteria was evident in people who knew next to nothing about OD. There were early proponents of OD who, it is safe to say, possessed a great deal more in the way of enthusiasm than of skill. In the early days of OD there was an evangelistic fervor that turned people off. And there were some rash commitments that failed, reinforcing the suspicion of many that OD was a passing fancy—and the sooner it passed, the better. One well-known business firm adopted all of the spirit of OD so impetuously that it nearly went out of business. Human relations is not an end in itself for a manufacturing concern.

These days OD has been successful—thanks to serious work by qualified, knowledgeable professionals—in purging itself of being known as a threatening, strange approach. Bottom-line results have been achieved. And OD is not one approach, but many. The emphasis these days is not on making people happy or helping them feel good about working together. Rather, OD practitioners concentrate on how conditions can be changed to enable employees to work more nearly up to their capacity, to make it possible for employees to achieve their goals and satisfaction by committing themselves to attainment of organizational goals.

OD consultants, from within or outside the organization, are called upon to design training and development programs, to help resolve interpersonal and intergroup conflicts, to advise on staffing and the structuring of work groups, to conduct diagnoses of operations in order to make recommendations for improvement of performance, to give their attention, in fact, to just about every aspect of an organization concerning people.

The theory base for OD, of course, is the work that has been described in this book. The efforts of thousands of OD practitioners in this country and abroad will continue to build on this base and to provide empirical evidence that the concern for individual human values, goals, and satisfaction is a legitimate, profitable investment for any kind of organization.

# Bibliography

Argyris, Chris. *Integrating the Individual and the Organization*. New York: John Wiley & Sons, 1964.

————. *Personality and Organization*. New York: Harper & Row, 1957.

Bennis, Warren G., and Slater, Philip E. *The Temporary Society*. New York: Harper & Row, 1968.

Berne, Eric. *Games People Play*. New York: Grove Press, 1964.

Blake, Robert R., and Mouton, Jane S. *The Managerial Grid*. Houston: Gulf Publishing Company, 1964.

Drucker, Peter F. *Management: Tasks, Responsibilities, Practices*. New York: Harper & Row, 1973.

————. *Managing for Results*. New York: Harper & Row, 1964.

Festinger, Leon. *Conflict, Decision and Dissonance*. Palo Alto: Stanford University Press, 1964.

Fiedler, Fred E. *A Theory of Leadership Effectiveness*. New York: McGraw-Hill Book Company, 1967.

Herzberg, Frederick: *The Motivation to Work*. New York: John Wiley & Sons, Inc., 1959.

————. *Work and the Nature of Man*. Cleveland: World Publishing Company, 1966.

Humble, John: *How to Manage by Objectives*. New York: American Management Association, 1973.

James, Muriel, and Jongeward, Dorothy. *Born to Win*. Reading: Addison-Wesley Publishing Company, 1971.

Lesieur, Frederick G., ed. *The Scanlon Plan: A Frontier in Labor-Management Cooperation*. New York: John Wiley & Sons, Inc., 1958.

Likert, Rensis. *The Human Organization*. New York: McGraw-Hill Book Company, 1967.

Marrow, Alfred J. *The Practical Theorist—The Life and Work of Kurt Lewin*. New York: Basic Books, 1969.

Maslow, Abraham H. *Motivation and Personality*. New York: Harper & Row, 1970.

McClelland, David. *The Achieving Society*. Princeton: Van Nostrand, 1961.

McGregor, Douglas. *The Human Side of Enterprise*. New York: McGraw-Hill Book Company, 1960.

Napier, Rodney W., and Gershenfeld, Matti K. *Groups: Theory and Experience*. Boston: Houghton Mifflin Company, 1973.

Odiorne, George S. *Management by Objectives*. New York: Pitman Publishing Corp., 1965.

Perls, Frederick, Hefferline, Ralph F., and Goodman, Paul. *Gestalt Therapy*. New York: Dell Publishing Co., Inc., 1951.

Roethlisberger, Fritz J., and Dickson, William J. *Management and the Worker*. Cambridge, Harvard University Press, 1939.

Rotter, Julian B., Chance, June E., and Phares, E. Jerry. *Applications of a Social-Learning Theory of Personality*. New York: Holt Rinehart Winston, 1972.

Skinner, B.F., and Holland, James G. *The Analysis of Behavior,* New York: McGraw-Hill Book Company, 1961.

Vroom, Victor H. *Worker and Motivation*. New York: John Wiley & Sons, Inc., 1964.

# Index

Hawthorne
  Effect, 5, 9
  experiments, 3–10, 91
  Works of Western Electric
    Company, 3
Herzberg, Frederick, 10, 21–26,
    34–35, 39, 43
  dissatisfiers, 22–24
  hygiene factors, *see*
    Dissatisfiers
  job enrichment, 24, 38–42
  *Motivation to Work, The,* 21
  motivators, *see* Satisfiers
  satisfiers, 21–24
  two-factor theory, 21–24, 39, 43
  *Work and the Nature of Man,* 21
Hidden agenda, 110–11
Hierarchy of needs, 13–17
Horizontal loading, 40
Hot seat, 66
Hughes, Charles L., 126–27
*Human Side of Enterprise, The,* 17
Humble, John, 42
Hygiene factor, *see* Dissatisfiers;
    Maintenance factors

Informal groups, 5–9

James, Muriel, 78
Job
  enlargement, 39
  enrichment, 24, 38–42
  rotation, 39
Jongeward, Dorothy, 78

Laboratory
  cousin, 97, 99
  family, 97
  instrumented, 99–100
  public, 99
  stranger, 99
  team-building, 99–100
Laissez-faire leadership, 117
Leadership
  autocratic, 117
  democratic, 117
  laissez-faire, 117

Learning, experiential, 101
Least-preferred co-worker, 125
Lewin, Kurt, 58–59, 63, 91–93,
    100, 117
Life positions, 81
Likert, Rensis, 123, 133–38, 140,
    144
Linking pins, 137–38
Loading
  horizontal, 40
  vertical, 40
Lose-lose, 85

McClelland, David C., 50–51
McGregor, Douglas, 10, 17–21,
    25, 118, 135
Maintenance factors, 22–24
Management
  benevolent authoritative, 134
  by objectives, 42–48
  consultative, 134
  contingency, 124–26
  Existential, 126–28
  exploitative authoritarian, 134
  participative, 133
Managerial Grid, 117–24
  seminar, 124
Maslow, Abraham H., 10, 13–17,
    19, 21, 24–25, 34
Matrix organization, 138, 139–41
Mayo, Elton, 3, 6
Method, group, 93, 102
Mirror manager, 127
Money
  as motivator, 23–24, 34–35
  as reward, 35
Morton, Robert B., 82, 83
*Motivation and Personality,* 13
*Motivation To Work, The,* 21
Motivators, *see* Satisfiers
Mouton, Jane S., 117, 124
Myers, M. Scott, 39

National Training Laboratories, 93

Obstructive group activities,
    111–12